THE BRITISH
Royal Family
GREAT FRONT PAGES

Introduced by
ANTHONY HOLDEN

Newspapers reproduced from the John Frost Historic Newspaper Service.

The Vendome Press
New York and Paris
1983

Designed and produced
for William Collins, Sons & Co. Ltd.
by Nutshell Ltd.
Typesetting by Eclipse Graphics Ltd.
Set in ITC Garamond
Printed and bound in Great Britain.

ISBN 0-86565-041-1

CONTENTS

INTRODUCTION
by Anthony Holden

"The *Daily Express*," said Prince Philip in 1962, "is a bloody awful newspaper". Next day the paper ran a Giles cartoon of its proprietor, Lord Beaverbrook, being frogmarched into the Tower of London by a posse of Beefeaters. "Ah well," Beaverbrook was consoling himself, "at least he takes it, or he wouldn't know it was a bloody awful newspaper."

It was not clear quite what had upset Philip so; his outburst came 15 years before, for instance, the *Express* "officially" married off his son Charles to Princess Marie-Astrid of Luxembourg. And today, if you visit either Prince at Buckingham Palace, the *Daily Express* is one of the two newspapers left for your edification in the waiting room at the Privy Purse entrance.

But the episode neatly distils the mutual suspicion which still prevails between British Royalty and British press: guarded hostility from the Throne, cautious cheekiness from Fleet Street. The press is not always as respectful as the Royal Family would like it to be; the Royal Family is neither as accessible nor as impervious to criticism as the press feels it should be.

The *Express* of the early 60s is not, perhaps, a typical example: Beaverbrook's personal feud with Philip's uncle, Lord Mountbatten, was an unusually stormtoss'd episode in the history of Palace-Fleet Street relations. Beaverbrook the Empire loyalist blamed Mountbatten the former Viceroy for "giving away India"; and Beaverbrook the Canadian blamed Mountbatten the former naval chief for his role in the 1942 Dieppe Landings, in which 3,000 Canadians died.

Royal revenge was taken in a rather unusual way: at one point in *In Which We Serve*, the film version of Mountbatten's wartime exploits aboard HMS Kelly, a copy of the *Daily Express* is seen awash in a gutter, proclaiming Beaverbrook's rash pre-war slogan: "There will be no war this year or next year."

In 1947, when the engagement of Prince Philip and Princess Elizabeth had yet to be announced, there was genuine fear in Royal circles that the Beaverbrook press would capitalise on anti-German sentiment against the Battenberg family, and oppose his naturalisation as Lieutenant Philip Mountbatten RN. Lord Louis invited the then editors of the *Daily Express* and *Sunday Express*, Arthur Christiansen and John Gordon, to his home for drinks, and won them round behind Beaverbrook's back. When their boss found out, he was furious: "Three tough old warhorses outmanoeuvred like that?"

So the Royals are as capable of editorial skulduggery as the most devious of politicians. Occasionally, too, they can use what might be called *force-majesté*: on several occasions all the national newspaper editors have been summoned to Buckingham Palace to be harangued. When Prince Charles first went to school, for instance, the editors were told that unless they called off their dogs, this great Royal educational experiment would be abandoned — and it would be the fault of the British press. They were suitably abashed.

The Palace handles such occasions cunningly. For a start, they don't convene them too often, thus devaluing them: there have been only three such gatherings during the present reign. The "pep talk" is delivered by the Queen's press secretary, and the monarch herself then appears to charm the editors into corgi-like obedience over a drink or two. It never fails.

Fleet Street editors rarely meet as a group — let alone behind a row of schoolroom-like desks, each with a little crested notepad. Like all their readers, they are reduced to utterly compliant jelly by the prospect of sharing a cocktail with the Queen. And like all men in high places, they earnestly wish to avoid doing anything which might endanger their knighthoods. So it was another triumph for Palace politics when they were all summoned in the Spring of 1982, and told to leave the then pregnant Princess of Wales in peace.

On that occasion, there was an unexpected bonus. During the cocktail session, the then editor of the *News of the World*, Barry Askew, asked the Queen why the Princess could not send out a servant to buy the wine gums she so craved. "Mr Askew," said his sovereign , "that is one of the most pompous remarks I have ever heard."

Newspaper editors and proprietors have also played more than minor roles in the recent history of the British monarchy. The most obvious example is the long and tortuous saga of King Edward VIII's relationship with an American divorcee, Mrs Wallis Simpson, which led to his abdication in December 1936. It was again Lord Beaverbrook at the centre of things, liaising personally with King and Prime Minister as he organised a conspiracy of silence in the British press about matters long since splashed all over American and continental newspapers. The one editor always threatening to break ranks, Geoffrey Dawson of *The Times*, finally unleashed a devastating editorial, inspired by dissident politicians, and arguing the case against the King.

In terms of sheer news values the abdication must rate as one of the "great" newspaper stories of this century. Many have condemned the hypocrisy of the press for agreeing to suppress the King's affair so long, then asking sundry awkward questions of the government on behalf of its baffled and angry readers. Once the news was out, this was certainly one Royal saga when neither Downing Street nor the Palace managed to have the coverage all its own way.

But there is a specific type of Royal occasion when Crown and Press are always instinctively at one: the great State occasion — a birth, a visit, a wedding, a death — when it is part of the British way of life, almost part of the constitution, that all other national affairs are swept aside. Royal engagements, weddings and births are as good for newspaper circulations as they are for the continuity and stability of the institution of monarchy; and so it is inevitably that they have generated many of the historic front pages contained in this collection. Death too is a great spur for newspaper drama: a time for solemn portraits to preside over black-bordered eulogies.

Many of the Queen's loyal subjects keep Royal scrapbooks, a practice dating back to the early years covered by this volume, when every outing by Queen Victoria was good for pious provincial coverage. Newspaper bosses are well aware of this, and the glossy souvenir editions published on great occasions are nothing new. Recent years have produced a spate of such events, to the delight of newspaper circulation managers: the Queen's Silver Jubilee in 1977, the engagement of Prince Charles to Lady Diana Spencer in 1981, their wedding that summer, and the birth of Prince William the following year.

The obsessive interest in Royalty generated by these kind of national events has been ever thus. When the ill-fated King Edward VIII was Prince of Wales in the 1920s-30s, he was quite as dashing and popular a figure as is the present Princess of Wales. Like her a leader of fashion, he later said that he had often wondered whether to the press he was not merely "a glorified clothes-peg". But these were the days before the electronic media, the zoom lens, the local radio station, the vast expansion of newspaper and broadcasting outlets with which the Palace's small team of press officers must cope.

They are, in the best sense of the word, "amateurs" — diplomats and ex-media men — rather than Madison Avenue or Saatchi and Saatchi "image-makers". The 1981 Royal Wedding was, quite simply, the biggest media event of all time, yet press coverage was organised by a diplomat on secondment from the Foreign Office, who happens also to be a prolific novelist — Michael Shea, the Queen's present press secretary. He managed, astonishingly, to publish three books the same year.

Of his early years, the Duke of Windsor recalled "with wonder and appreciation the ease with which we were able to move about in public places . . . Because our likeness seldom appeared in the press, we were not often recognised on the street; when we were, the salutation would be a friendly wave of the hand, or a polite lifting of the hat." The childhood of Charles, his successor as Prince of Wales, was very different. His nannies frequently had to abandon attempts to walk him through London's parks, and one of his first skiing holidays was described as "like a scene from a Keystone cops movie . . . impatient voices bawled suggestions in English, French, Italian and German, their cars revving madly, wheels spinning, as they leaped, slithered and bumped into each other in a frantic race for the best positions behind the speeding sleighs."

In the ensuing quarter-century press harassment of the Royals has only, as we all know, got worse. Some members of the present Royal Family are better with the press than others: Charles and Diana, for instance, have never (like Princess Anne) sworn at photographers, nor (like Prince Philip) turned a hose on them. But they have come close.

After the bitter mutual recriminations of 1982-3, it seems likely that the most assiduous of Fleet Street's self-styled "Royal-watchers" will realise that it is in their interests to stop short of wholesale invasion of Royal privacy.

On the other hand, as Prince Charles himself said: "In my sort of job, it's when nobody wants to write about you or take a photograph of you that you ought to be worrying. Then there'd be no great point in being around."

CHAPTER 1

QUEEN VICTORIA & EDWARD VII

*She had little to do with the press,
which is one way of remaining a popular monarch.*

The *Sun* has changed a bit since 1838, when an Ode to the new Queen by one Murdo Young embellished a special Coronation supplement, price one penny. There was no Page Three girl, and Victoria's coronation robes were valued at a super, soaraway £4 10s 6d.

In those days the *Sun* was a London evening paper, a rival to the *Standard* still with us today, which reported the funeral of Prince Albert, in 1861, with heavy black borders around its columns.

Queen Victoria had little to do with the press, which is of course one way of remaining a popular monarch. She was especially loved by the provincial papers, who reported the second attempt on her life, four years after her coronation, in appalled tones. "It was hard to believe," wrote the *Bury and Norwich Post*, "that *two* persons could be found in this kingdom so dead to the feelings, not only of loyalty but of humanity, as to be capable of so execrable a deed…"

And the *Nottinghamshire Guardian* waxed lyrical, in a special "fine art" supplement, over her diamond jubilee: "The monarchy is more firmly established than ever in the confidence and affections of the British people, and the Imperial flag floats over the most glorious empire in the annals of all time… The Queen has swayed her sceptre during a period of unexampled progress in the pacific arts, of splendid achievement in commerce and industry, of remarkable advance in the realms of science."

Then as now, most Royal news was good. Victoria herself may have been mourning for her beloved Albert, but the marriage of her son Bertie, the popular Prince of Wales, to a beautiful Danish Princess called Alexandra in 1863 had the nation enthralled, as did the sequence of Royal births which followed. Apart from Bertie himself, three more future British Kings were to be born during Victoria's reign — though none would realise then that the grandson named after Bertie would one day himself inherit the throne after his elder

brother's abdication.

It is not only in recent years that big Royal events have been good news for newspaper circulation managers. In 1863, as in 1981, a host of special supplements were available to celebrate the Royal nuptials. *Plus ça change.*

The 12-page, sixpenny Royal Marriage Number of the *Illustrated Times* offered engravings of Alexandra's family, even her birthplace, as well as artists' impressions of her triumphal progress through London. The text set out the route in meticulous detail, printed the order of the wedding service, and offered many a historical parallel. On the back page, the Danish National Anthem and "D'Albert's Prince of Wales's Galop" were among the sheet music offered for sale, at four and three shillings respectively, in the crowded and lucrative columns of classified adverts.

But bad news, it has to be said, can be equally profitable. Victoria's death in January 1901 was the signal for a spate of dramatically funeral front pages, all bearing solemn "last portraits" of Britain's longest-reigning monarch. "The best-loved sovereign who ever ruled the destinies of the British Empire," wrote the *Illustrated Mail,* (p.8), a weekly supplement to the *Daily Mail,* "has gone to her rest."

Inside the "Empire in Mourning" edition of the *Daily Graphic* (p.9), you could buy a 65-day Royal Mail Line cruise around all the islands of the West Indies for £65, or rent a flat in London's West End (with garden and tennis court) for £36 a year.

The Edwardian era quickly dispelled the public gloom. Victoria had anyway been a reclusive monarch for many years, and the popular Bertie's arrival on the throne pitched the country into a joyous and stylish decade.

The reports of his Derby win (p.11) and his rumbustious social life (p.12) capture the high spirits of a lusty but all too short era. Only nine years after succeeding his mother, after waiting sixty, King Edward too was staring solemnly from the front page of an In Memoriam edition of the *Daily Mirror.*

The Sun.

WITH WHICH THE "TRUE SUN" IS NOW INCORPORATED.

No. 14,289. LONDON, THURSDAY EVENING, JUNE 28, 1838. PRICE 1s.

God Save

Victoria R.

THE CORONATION.

Mr. Thompson, in his work on The Processions and Ceremonies observed in the Coronation of the Kings and Queens of England, gives the following account of

KING EDWARD'S CHAIR.

"This chair (commonly called St. Edward's chair) is an ancient seat of solid, hard wood, with back and sides of the same, variously painted, in which the kings of Scotland were in former periods constantly crowned: but, having been brought out of the kingdom by King Edward I., in the year 1296, after he had totally overcome John Baliol king of Scots, it has ever since remained in the abbey of Westminster, and has been the royal chair in which the succeeding kings and queens of this realm have been inaugurated. It is in height 6 ft. 7 in., in breadth at the bottom, 38 in., and in depth 24 in.: from the seat to the bottom is 25 in., the breadth of the seat within the sides is 28 in., and the depth 18 in. At 9 inches from the ground is a board, supported at the four corners by as many lions. Between the seat and this board is enclosed a stone, commonly called Jacob's, or the Fatal Marble Stone, which is an oblong, of about 22 in. in length, 13 in. broad, and 11 in. deep; of a steel colour, mixed with some veins of red. History relates that it is the stone whereon the patriarch Jacob laid his head in the plain of Luz. It is also added that it was brought to Brigantia, in the kingdom of Gallicia in Spain, in which place Gathol king of Scots, sat on it as his throne. Thence it was conveyed into Ireland by Simon Brach, who was king of Scots, about 700 years before Christ's time; from thence into Scotland by king Fergus, about 370 years afterwards; and, in the year 850, it was placed in the abbey of Scone, in the sheriffdom of Perth, by King Kenneth, who caused it to be enclosed in this wooden chair, and a phophetical verse to be engraved, of which the following is a translation:

'Should fate not fail, where'er this stone is found
The Scots shall monarchs of that realm be crown'd.'

"This is the more remakable by its having been fulfilled in the person of King James I., grandfather to the Princess Sophia, electress dowager of Hanover, grandmother to King George II., who was grandfather to his late Majesty, George III. This antique regal chair, having (together with the golden sceptre and crown of Scotland) been solemnly offered by King Edward I. to St. Edward the Confessor, in the year 1297 (from whence it derives the appellation of St. Edward's chair), has ever since been kept in the chapel called by his name: with a tablet affixed to it, whereon several Latin verses are written in the old English characters. The ornaments of this chair consist of crockets and fret-work, richly gilt. It has a cushion, covered with the same materials. The stone maintains its usual place under the seat of the chair, but is hid from observation by the fringe which surrounds it."

THE REGALIA.

These are—St. Edward's Staff—the Spurs—the Sceptre with the Cross—the Pointed Sword of Temporal Justice—the Sword of Mercy—the Sword of State—the Sceptre with the Dove—the Orb—St. Edward's Crown—the Patina, the Chalice, and the Bible.

St. Edward's Staff, in length four feet eleven inches and a half, is a sceptre of gold, having a foot of steel about four inches and a quarter in length, with a mound and cross at the top; the ornaments are also of gold, and the diameter is upwards of three-quarters of an inch.

The Spurs, called the great golden Spurs, are elaborately wrought; they have no rowels, but end in an ornamented point.

The Sceptre with the Cross, or Sceptre Royal, is likewise of gold, the handle plain, and the upper part wreathed; it is in length two feet nine inches and a quarter, and is of the same thickness as the former. The point at the lower part is enriched with rubies, emeralds, and small diamonds: and the space of five inches and a half in length, above the handle, is elegantly embellished with similar precious stones. The top rises into a fleur-de-lis, with six leaves, of which three are upright, and the other three are hanging down, all enriched with precious stones; out of the fleur-de-lis issues a mound made of an amethyst, set round with table-diamonds, and upon the mound a cross, wholly covered with precious stones, and a large table-diamond in the centre.

The Sword of Justice of the Temporality, or Third Sword, is sharp-pointed; the length of the handle is four inches, the pommel an inch and three-quarters, and the cross seven inches and a half; the scabbard in all respects is like the two former.

Curtoma, or the Pointless Sword, representing the Sword of Mercy, is the principal in dignity of three swords which are borne naked before the kings at the coronation. It is a broad bright sword, of which the length of the blade is thirty-two inches, the breadth almost two inches, the handle, which is covered with fine gold wire is four inches long, and the pommel an inch and three-quarters, which, with the cross, is plain steel gilt, the length of the cross is almost eight inches. The scabbard belonging to it is covered with a rich brocaded cloth of tissue, with gilt ornaments.

The sword of state, which is a large two-handed sword, having a splendid scabbard of crimson velvet, decorated with gold plates of the royal badges, in order as follow:—Up at the point is the orb or mound, then the royal crest of a lion standing on an imperial crown; lower down are a portcullis, harp, thistle, fleur-de-lis, and rose; near the hilt is the portcullis repeated; next are the royal arms and supporters; and, lastly, the harp, thistle, &c., occur over again. The other side of the scabbard is exactly the same. The handle and pommel of the sword are embossed with similar devices in silver gilt; and the cross is formed of the royal supporters, the lion and unicorn, having a rose within a laurel between them on one side, and a fleur-de-lis, encircled in the same manner, on the other.

The king's sceptre with the dove is a sceptre of gold, in length three feet seven inches, three inches in circumference at the handle, and two inches and a quarter round the top. The pommel is decorated with a circle or fillet of table-diamonds, and in several places with precious stones of all sorts, and the mound at the top is embellished with a band or fillet of rose-diamonds. Upon the mount is a small Jerusalem cross, wherein is fixed a dove with wings expanded, as the emblem of mercy.

The orb, mound, or globe, is a ball of gold of six inches diameter, encompassed with a band of the same, embellished with roses of diamonds encircling other precious stones, and edged about with pearl. On the top is a very large amethyst, of a violet or purple colour, near an inch and a half in height, of an oval form, and which, being encompassed with four silver wires, becomes the pedestal of a splendid cross of gold of three inches and a quarter in height and three inches in breadth, set very close with diamonds, having, in the middle, a sapphire on one side, and an emerald on the other. It is also embellished with four large pearls in the angles of the cross, near the centre, and three more at the ends of it. The whole height of the orb and cross is eleven inches.

The first and principal diadem, denominated St. Edward's Crown, with which his Majesty is invested, is so called in commemoration of the ancient one, which was kept in Westminster Abbey till the beginning of the great rebellion, when, with the rest of the regalia, it was sacrilegiously carried away. It is a very rich imperial crown, embellished with pearls and precious stones of various kinds, as diamonds, rubies, emeralds, and sapphires, with a mound of gold on the top of it, encircled with a band of the same, embellished also with precious stones; and upon the mound a cross of gold decorated in a similar manner, having three very large oval pearls, one at the top of the cross, and two others pendant at the sides of it. This crown is composed, as all those of England are, of four crosses and as many fleur-de-lis upon a rim or circle of gold, all embellished with precious stones, from the tops of which crosses arise four circular bars or arches, which meet at the top, and at the intersection is the pedestal whereon is fixed the mound. The cap within the crown is of purple velvet lined with white taffeta and turned up with ermine, thickly powdered in three rows.

THE AMPULLA AND ANOINTING SPOON.

The ampulla, which contains the holy oil, is in the form of an eagle, with the wings expanded, standing on a pedestal, all of pure gold, finely chased. The head unscrews at the middle of the neck for the convenience of putting in the oil, and, the vessel being entirely hollow, it is poured out into the spoon through the point of the beak. The weight of the whole is nearly eight or ten ounces, and the cavity of the body is capable of containing about six ounces. The anointing spoon is likewise of pure gold, with four pearls set in the broadest part of handle: the bowl of the spoon is finely chased both within and without, and, by its extreme thinness, appears to be very ancient.

THE CORONATION DAY.

BY MURDO YOUNG.

All hail, Queen Victoria! all hail to this day,
So teeming with promise—we welcome it here
As the bright stream of glory pursues its glad way,
And the blessing of thousands ascends in that cheer!

But if thousands on thousands are happy before thee,
Saluting thy favours, and catching thy smiles:
Oh! think of the millions of hearts that adore thee—
For this day is a JUBILEE over the isles!

Not alone o'er the isles—but Hindostan afar
Doth *our* jubilee spread—in the West, the poor slave,
As he prays for thy mercy, "fair Liberty's star!
"Be the Queen of the FREE, as the Queen of the brave.

Let the African joy, for his freedom is nigh;
Our Queen would not reign but o'er happy and free:
Let that thunder attest it—yon banner on high—
The Banner of Glory o'er land and o'er sea!

Bear witness, ye Nations! the homage we pay,
The pride that we feel, and the love we declare:
For the Queen of our hearts is, on this happy day,
Not alone of the brave—but THE Queen of the Fair!

Nor can chivalry boast, in the rolls of renown,
A scene such as THIS—for old Time stands apart,
While the Crown of her PEOPLE VICTORIA puts on,
All radiant with beauty—and pure as her heart!

Then fill up a bumper to honour THE QUEEN!
Our hands and our hearts in devotion we give:
And our children, while weeping with joy o'er this scene,
Shall pray, GOD bless VICTORIA! and long may she live.

SKETCH OF HER MAJESTY.

Her most gracious Majesty is the only daughter of the duke of Kent, the fourth son of George III., and of the duchess of Kent the sister of Leopold, king of the Belgians. She was born on the 24th of May, 1819, and had reached the age (eighteen) required by the law, before she could assume the reins of government, in the month previous to her accession to the throne on the death of William the Reformer, on June 20th, 1837. On the present memorable day her Majesty was crowned, and now reigns over an affectionate and trusting people by all possible legal titles.

Till her accession to the throne her Majesty led a retired life under the care of her mother, who, giving up her native land, devoted herself most assiduously to the education of her child, in order to make her Majesty worthy of the high station to which she was born.

During the short time her Majesty has reigned she has well responded to the "tender and enlightened mother," under whose care, her Majesty said, "I have learned from my infancy to respect and love the constitution of my native country." On her first memorable appearance before the Council on the day of her accession, "stepping from the privacy of domestic life to the discharge of her high functions," she so demeaned herself as to cause general approbation. "She inspired," said Sir Robert Peel, "a confident expectation that she was destined to a reign of happiness for her people and of glory to herself." "There is something," he added, "which art cannot make nor lessons teach, and can only be suggested by a high and generous nature." Her Majesty has completely realised the hopes with which her careful education and her demeanour on her accession to the throne inspired all her subjects.

Her Majesty has always willingly met her people, and on both occasions she opened and closed the Parliament in person. One of the most memorable events since her accession was the great festival given to her by the City of London in November last year, which her Majesty honoured with her presence.

All who have had occasion to approach her Majesty speak with delight of her condescension and affability, and no deserving object of the royal bounty ever applied to her Majesty in vain.

Of her Majesty's personal appearance we need not speak, as the splendid portrait above gives more information at a glance than we could convey in a column. We may observe, however, that her Majesty is not tall, though she is graceful in her movements.

Her Majesty is said to be a good musician, and to be well versed in modern languages as well as in those sciences, such as botany, which are suitable for an an accomplished lady. She has shown herself, since her accession to the throne, a generous patron of the theatres and the fine arts, and has already done much to restore them in England to the splendour of the Elizabethan age. Men of science have not been overlooked, and England promises to be as celebrated under her reign for the peaceful arts as ever it was for warlike deeds under the most renowned of her predecessors.

Her reign has been already distinguished by the establishment of a regular communication by steam with the United States, and the rapid improvements now continually made in the arts, of which our journal this day presents one splendid specimen, betoken an unprecedented progress in civilization. For her Majesty's reign to be glorious for herself and happy for her people, her political measures must correspond with the extraordinary movement now impelled on society. Following a monarch who acquired a deservedly-high reputation as a reformer, her task, and the task of her statesmen, it must be admitted, is not easy. But those who see in all things the directing hand of Providence will probably look on the graces of a female reign as likely to temper most advantageously the character of the monarchy, which, in this age of the world and with the present temper of mankind, might be exposed to much risk were either a heartless debauchée or a wilful tyrant to be on the throne.

Illustrated Mail.

THE WEEKLY EDITION OF THE DAILY MAIL.

VOL. II.—NO. 85.   [REGISTERED AT THE G.P.O.   LONDON, JANUARY 26, 1901.   AS A NEWSPAPER.]   ONE PENNY.

THE EMPIRE MOURNS ITS LOSS.

[Photograph by Downey.

SMOKE . . .
Tortoise=shell Mixture

THE DAILY GRAPHIC
ONE PENNY

LONDON : TUESDAY, FEBRUARY 5, 1901.

No. 3,471.—Vol. XLV.

REGISTERED AS A NEWSPAPER

THE QUEEN'S FUNERAL.

LAST SAD RITES.

INTERMENT AT FROGMORE.

ANOTHER IMPRESSIVE PAGEANT.

The interment of the Queen's remains at Frogmore yesterday was marked by another picturesque pageant and an affecting final service. These formed at once a marked contrast and an impressive sequel to the memorable proceedings of last week. This concluding stage of the historic ceremonial did not, of course, take the form of a popular demonstration. There was no longer the pressure of vast crowds, and no glittering array of Ambassadors or statesmen, but there was still much to stir every imagination. Since the funeral service in St. George's Chapel on Saturday, the Royal coffin has remained, under constant guard, in the Albert Memorial Chapel, where the tombs of the Duke of Clarence and the Duke of Albany are conspicuous among other costly and artistic memorials of departed Royalty. The public were excluded from the Castle yard, and even the Military Knights of Windsor had to keep such visitors as they received within the boundary of their own dwellings along the outer side of the lower ward.

IN THE CASTLE YARD.

At half-past two o'clock the red-coated squad of selected coffin-bearers arrived within the enclosure. They consisted of two stalwart Lifeguards, with brass helmets and white plumes, and eight or ten Foot Guards. Soon after they had passed within the chapel, the instrumental bands of the 2nd Life Guards and the Grenadier Guards arrived and passed on to the Upper Ward in readiness to take their appointed rank in the procession. They were followed by the Queen's company of the Grenadier Guards, who were formed up in line upon the grassy slope on the southern side of the pathway. Among the picturesque figures who shortly appeared upon the scene were the late Queen's two pipers, Mr. James Campbell and his nephew, in full Highland costume. Near them gathered another Scotch kilted group. Many spectators took them also for pipers, but they were foresters and stalkers from the Royal domain at Balmoral. As the time approached for the procession to form, several Court functionaries, in Windsor uniform, arrived and busied themselves in giving directions. The gun-carriage, drawn by eight horses of the Royal Artillery, was brought up and placed between the line of soldiers and the chapel. Meantime the surpliced choir, headed by Sir Walter Parratt, in his academic hood, passed up the yard on their way to Frogmore, in advance of the procession. The robed clergy now came upon the scene. The Bishop of Winchester and the Dean of Windsor took their stand near the Lord Steward and the Lord Chamberlain, at the Chapel door. At five minutes to three o'clock the Royal party

arrived on foot from the Castle, and were, of course, greeted with a Royal salute. The King, who was in the uniform of a Field Marshal, covered with a dark cloak, walked alone. He was followed by the German Emperor, the Duke of Connaught, the King of Portugal, and the other Royal and Princely personages who have been his guests. Then came the Queen and other Royal ladies, all in deep mourning and thickly veiled. Her Majesty led by the hand her little grandson, Prince Edward, who was dressed in sailor costume. The King and his party stood outside the entrance to the chapel, and there was a brief interval of silence, broke only by the solemn tolling of bells and the boom of the minute-gun, fired some distance away in the grounds by a battery of artillery. At three o'clock punctually the coffin was slowly borne out of the chapel and placed with reverence upon the gun-carriage, after which the rich white silk pall, with the crown and other emblems of Sovereignty, was placed upon the coffin.

THE PROCESSION.

The gallant Grenadiers marched at slow step to the Upper Ward in the rear of their band, the clergy took their places, the chief Court officials placed themselves in position, and at the word of command the procession slowly moved off to the mournful strains of Chopin's "Marche Funèbre," played with touching effect. The following was the order of the procession :—

The Queen's Company of Grenadier Guards, with reversed arms.
The Duke of Argyll, K.G., K.T., Governor of Windsor Castle.
Highland Pipers.
Royal Servants.
Band of the Grenadier Guards.
The Bishop of Winchester.

The Dean of Windsor.
The Lord Chamberlain.
The Lord Steward.

AT SIDE OF COFFIN.		AT SIDE OF COFFIN.
Lieut.-Col. A. Davidson, M.V.O.		Col. J. Brocklehurst, M.V.O
Lieut.-Col. Hon. H. C. Legge, M.V.O.	GUN CARRIAGE	Capt. F. Ponsonby, M.V.O.
Lieut.-Col. Sir A. Bigge, K.C.B., C.M.G.		Lieut.-Col. Hon. W. P. Carington, C.B.
Major-General Sir J. M'Neill, V.C., K.C.B., K.C.M.G.		Lieut.-Col. the Right Hon. Sir Fleetwood Edwards, K.C.B.

Maj. Count Gleichen, C.M.G.
THE KING.
The German Emperor.
The King of the Belgians.
The King of Portugal.
The Duke of Connaught.
Prince Henry of Prussia.

(Continued on page 3.)

THE FUNERAL PAGEANT AT SPITHEAD: THE KING AND THE KAISER ON THE BRIDGE OF THE ROYAL YACHT VICTORIA AND ALBERT.

BASINGSTOKE
CORONATION SUPPLEMENT
TO
The Hampshire Observer.

SATURDAY, AUGUST 16, 1902.　　　　[Gratis with Paper.

His Majesty King Edward VII.

Her Majesty Queen Alexandra.

HOW BASINGSTOKE KEPT THE CORONATION.

SUCCESSFUL AND ENTHUSIASTIC CELEBRATION.

' I'm determined that Basingstoke shall come to the front yet; we will not be behind the rest of Hampshire,' remarked the gallant Mayor (Lieut.-Colonel May) at a meeting of the Coronation Committee a few weeks ago. Well, it has come to the front, for it may safely be asserted not only that nowhere in the King's dominions was Coronation Day more heartily observed, but also that there were very few places, if any, in Hampshire which came up to Basingstoke in the completeness of its Coronation celebrations. The proceedings throughout the day were alike worthy of the auspicious event, worthy of the old borough which has ever, even in the most troubled days of English history, been noted for its loyalty to the Throne, and a credit to Hampshire. The good people of Basingstoke are proud of the way in which they celebrated the Coronation, and they have every reason for their pride. Led by their worthy Mayor, who seems to have made his own the proud motto of the gallant defender of Basing House, ' Aymez loyaute,' they entered most heartily into the spirit of the day, and determined with his Worship that Basingstoke, far from being behind, should be well to the front. In the columns which follow we have set out as fully as possible the various details in a day replete with interest and pleasure, but it is impossible with pen and picture to fully describe all that the celebration was in Basingstoke. From early morning till midnight there was not a dull moment, and everything went off with the utmost enthusiasm. The thanksgiving service, the procession, the planting of the Coronation trees, the fete in the meadows, the children's tea, the concert by the Blue Viennese Band, and the torchlight procession, each and all can best be described in the one word—Success. The weather was dull at times, but the rain kept off, the streets were gaily decorated with flags and bunting, and at night were ablaze with illuminations, and altogether the old town has never presented such a gala appearance. It was matter for regret in one way that the Mayor was not able to be present during the early part of the day, as his personality always inspires enthusiasm, but the inhabitants proudly bore

the disappointment, because they knew that he was engaged in a higher duty in connection the borough in Westminster Abbey. And so well perfected had been the arrangements that everything worked smoothly and successfully under the genial supervision of the ex-Mayor (Councillor H. Jackson). The Mayor was back again early in the afternoon and at once took the lead, and thenceforward till the proceedings closed at midnight he was busily engaged.

In this Supplement we present our readers with, as far as possible, a complete record of a day which the oldest will remember with pride, and which the youngest will always look back to with pleasure.

THE MAYOR AND THE CORONATION.

The borough of Basingstoke is fortunate in having as its Mayor in the Coronation year such a warm-hearted and generous gentleman as Lieut.-Colonel May, whose life has been devoted to the welfare of his native town, and whose six mayoralties have been marked by a patriotism, a hospitality, and a philanthropy excelled by no other borough in the kingdom, even if it has been equalled, which is extremely doubtful. We need not here review the gallant Colonel's life history, as it was fully set forth in the Supplement with which we presented our readers on July 5th last, but it may be well, on this auspicious occasion, to briefly recall his fortuitous connection with royal events. He was born in the year in which Queen Victoria came to the throne (1837); he first entered the Corporation in the year of the marriage of our present beloved King and Queen (1863); he was mayor in the year of the late Queen's Jubilee (1887); again in the year of the Diamond Jubilee (1897), and now he has crowned his royal record by his Coronation mayoralty. Apart from princely contributions towards local festivities connected with each of these three great events in our national history, he has done something to permanently mark each event, and at the same time to confer a blessing and benefit on others. In 1887 he placed on the Town Hall the magnificent clock tower which is a landmark for miles round, and which stands as a type of his lifelong efforts for the uplifting of his fellow townsmen and the elevation of his native borough. In 1897 he built a wing to the Cottage Hospital, which is an outward and visible sign of his deep interest in the poor and afflicted, and his earnest endeavours to mitigate sorrow and suffering. And he has this year given further proof of this trait in his character, both in a national and a local manner. Early in this Coronation year he initiated a movement which was later on taken up by the Lord Mayor of London, for permanently commemorating the Coronation by a gift to King Edward's Hospital Fund, and on his initiative £50 from the local Coronation fund was devoted to that object, a sum which his Worship supplemented by £25 from his private purse. And now he has inaugurated as a thanksgiving for the King's restoration to health a shilling fund for the Basingstoke Cottage Hospital, which, like most other hospitals, is sadly in need of increased financial support. And in a smaller way he has left his impress on the Coronation year by presenting a number of seats to the recreation ground.

[Photo]　　　　[Chase, Southsea.

Basingstoke's Coronation Mayor
(Alderman Lieut.-Col. J. May, V.D., J.P.) in his Coronation Court Dress.

Of the gallant Mayor's more transitory kindly acts in connection with the Coronation it is impossible to speak in detail, for their name is legion, but we may mention a few of the principal. He started the local fund with fifty guineas from his own purse, and a similar amount from the coffers of Messrs. John May and Co., Limited; he has defrayed the whole cost of the splendid illuminations and decorations of the Town Hall, the Drill Hall, and the Corn Exchange; he engaged at his own expense the celebrated Blue Viennese Band on June 27th, and again last Saturday, and on the latter occasion he also paid for the Eastleigh Works Band, and his was the purse which provided the medals, about 4,000 in all, which were distributed to the school children, the Coronation Committee, the naval and military veterans, police, inmates of the almshouses, and others. Added to this he, during the semi-festivities on June 26th and 27th, and again on Saturday and Sunday, as well as at the peace celebration and the reception to Lord Kitchener, dispensed hospitality to large numbers of guests at the Town Hall, as well as giving some splendid entertainments at his private residence at Hawkfield.

Not many mayors in England have such a record in connection with the Coronation, and happy indeed is the borough which possesses such a mayor. No wonder then that the people of Basingstoke are proud of their Mayor, and indeed, whether in office or out of office, Colonel May is always popular with the inhabitants. It was therefore with intense joy that they heard last week that he had been invited to the Coronation in Westminster Abbey, and the honour, and well-deserved honour, thus conferred on the Mayor was reflected on the borough wherein his name is a household word.

THANKSGIVING SERVICE IN THE MARKET PLACE.

Very fitly the day's proceedings began with a united thanksgiving service in the Market-place. Six weeks before the inhabitants of all creeds and classes had gathered there to offer up their united intercessions to Almighty God that He would be pleased to spare the King and restore him to health, and now in the same spot, under the happiest possible auspices, they foregathered to unitedly thank God that He had brought His people to that day, and to pray that He would crown the King 'with all princely virtues.' It was a deeply impressive and picturesque scene, and, as on the previous occasion, the greatest reverence and heartiness was manifested. And Heaven smiled on the service, for as the prayers and praises proceeded the clouds, which hitherto had been black and lowering, lifted, and for a short space the sun shone out brilliantly, and lit up the picturesque scene. The arrangements were precisely the same as on that never to be forgotten evening at the end of June. The bandstand, which had been erected in the centre of the Market-place (beneath the Diamond Jubilee lamp), was improvised as a dais for the Corporation, the borough magistrates, and the representatives of the School Board. The Deputy Mayor (Councillor H. Jackson, J.P.) stood at the front of the civic body, facing the Town Hall, and was accompanied by Mrs. Gilbert Allen

10

THREE PAGES OF DERBY DAY PICTURES. (1, 8, and 9.)

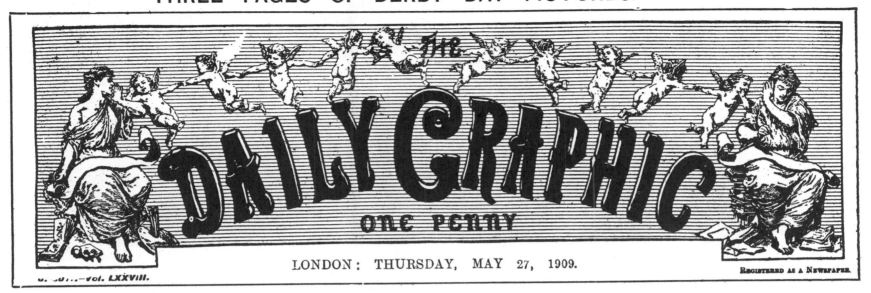

DAILY GRAPHIC
ONE PENNY

LONDON: THURSDAY, MAY 27, 1909.

Registered as a Newspaper.

No. 5817.—Vol. LXXVIII.

THE CROWN DERBY.

THE KING WATCHES MINORU COMING IN.

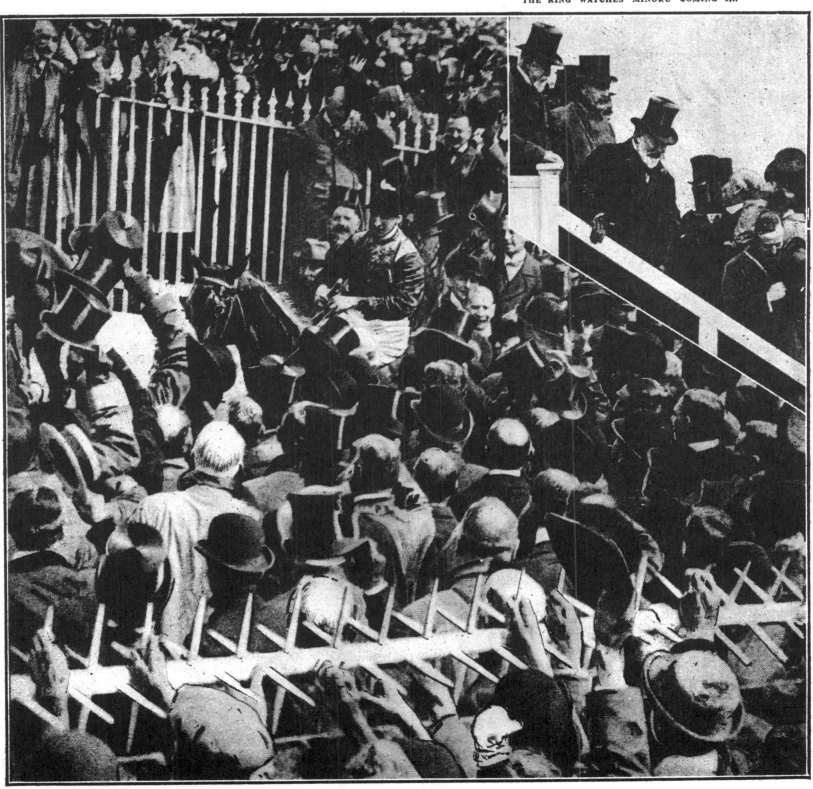

HIS MAJESTY'S MINORU RECEIVING A GREAT OVATION ON ENTERING THE WEIGHING-IN ENCLOSURE AFTER WINNING THE DERBY—THE FIRST IN HISTORY WON BY A SOVEREIGN—AT EPSOM YESTERDAY.

("Daily Graphic" Photograph.) (See page 7.)

DAILY SKETCH.

The ALL-PICTURE MORNING PAPER.

No. 98.   [Registered as a Newspaper.]   TUESDAY, JULY 6, 1909.   ONE HALFPENNY.

THE KING'S WEEK-END AT COTON HOUSE, RUGBY.

(1) The King; (2) Mrs. Arthur James; (3) the Duke of Richmond and Gordon; (4) Mr. Whitelaw Reid American Ambassador; (5) Mrs. George Keppel; (6) Mr. Arthur James; (7) the Earl of Durham; (8) Mrs. Willie James.

Mr. Arthur James.   The King in the grounds at Coton House.   Mrs. Arthur James.

The Queen, accompanied by Princess Victoria, left Euston at 9-55 yesterday morning by special train for Huyton, the station for Knowsley, where the King and Queen and the Princess are the guests of the Earl and Countess of Derby during their engagements in the North. The train stopped specially at Rugby, where the King passed the week-end at Coton House with Mr. and Mrs. Arthur James, whose house party is pictured above. Sunday was bright and sunny, and the house party motored to Churchover and attended divine service, Mrs. Arthur James playing the organ.

The Daily Mirror

THE MORNING JOURNAL WITH THE SECOND LARGEST NET SALE

No. 2,037. | Registered at the G. P. O. as a Newspaper. | SATURDAY, MAY 7, 1910 | One Halfpenny.

THE WORLD IN MOURNING: DEATH OF EDWARD THE PEACEMAKER, KING AND EMPEROR.

The King died during the night from an attack of bronchitis which had confined his Majesty to his room for three days. His Majesty, who was born on November 9, 1841, and was thus in his sixty-ninth year, had reigned since the death of Queen Victoria on January 22, 1901.

CHAPTER 2

GEORGE V

The King was never quite sure what his people thought of him.

After King Edward VII's death, Queen Alexandra retreated into seclusion at Sandringham. But her daughter-in-law, now Queen Mary, quickly took over from her that unique role in the nation's affections which belongs to a Queen Consort — and is still held today by the present Queen Mother.

All of them lived to ripe old ages. The present Queen Mother is as old as the century and still going strong. Alexandra was to die during her son's reign, in 1925, at the age of 80. Queen Mary outlived both of her sons who became King, and died only two months before Elizabeth II's coronation, aged 85.

Her husband's arrival on the throne in 1910 meant that British newspapers again had a young Royal Family to coo over — no fewer than five young Princes and one Princess. The *Daily Mirror,* in a special "Queen Mary number" (p.17), reported proudly how the young Princelings had "all been trained to love manly sports". But the baby the Queen holds in her arms, Prince John, was to lead a tragically short life marked by illness, and die at the age of 13 in 1919 (p.21).

Before the end of the reign, the papers were able to greet the beginnings of the next generation — for whom such an unexpected destiny lay in store. The King's daughter-in-law, the Duchess of York, gave birth to Princess Elizabeth in 1926 and Princess Margaret four years later (p.51). Any new picture of the young Princesses was always good for a whole front page (p.50).

At the beginning of George V's reign, the special coronation issues (p.15) of the pop papers of the day rivalled each other in splendour and special offers. Each coronation issue of the *Daily Graphic,* for instance, carried free insurance worth £1,000 in the event of death on public transport.

But newspaper proprietors were soon to have an added and unexpected bonus in the investiture of young Prince Edward — the future Duke of Windsor — as Prince of Wales at Caernarvon in 1911 (p.35). He was the first Prince of Wales in modern times to undergo the ordeal (as he himself called it), which was really a flagrantly vote-catching spectacular laid on by the Prime Minister, David Lloyd George. It set a precedent followed by the present Queen and her heir in 1969 (p. 119).

George V was a somewhat remote, rather stern figure for a 20th-Century monarch, who was never quite sure what his people thought of him. "I never realised they liked me for myself," he was to say to his Queen in 1935, surprised by the warmth of his Silver Jubilee celebrations. But he and Mary also conducted several highly successful overseas tours, notably to India in 1912 (p.18) and Italy in 1923 (p.23).

During the First World War the King was also copiously covered visiting his victorious troops in the field of battle (p.20). As in the Second World War, the monarch became to the press a symbol of national stability during the dark days of war — and the focal point of the national rejoicing at its end.

Another feature of the reign vividly reflected in the pages that follow was the remarkable publicity accorded the King's eldest son Edward, the glamorous young Prince of Wales and heir apparent. (Never, as things were to turn out, has the word 'apparent' been more appropriate.)

Edward — known to his family as David — cut a stylish figure at home and abroad. A kind of combination of Prince Charles and Prince Andrew — a future King who was nevertheless more than capable of risqué public behaviour — he was meat and drink to the national press.

When he went to South America, for instance, to open the Buenos Aires air show, the *Daily Sketch* thought it worth rushing pictures back in three days by "fast steamer" and aeroplane (p.37).

Another newspaper bonus of the reign, given so many Royal offspring, was a plethora of Royal weddings, all worth special editions. In retrospect, of course, the most notable is that of the King's second son, the Duke of York, to Lady Elizabeth Bowes-Lyon in 1923 (p.49). She had twice turned him down, for fear of marrying into even a junior branch of the Royal Family. Little did she know her husband would be reluctantly pitchforked onto the throne — and little did the nation know that it was witnessing the wedding of a future King and Queen.

For the romance which continued to go unreported, and became increasingly conspicuous by its absence, was that of the King's eldest son, the dashing and popular young Prince of Wales…

THE DAILY GRAPHIC, JUNE 23, 1911

£1,000   THIS ISSUE OF "THE DAILY GRAPHIC" CARRIES A FREE INSURANCE OF **£1,000** UNDER-   **£1,000**
TAKEN BY THE OCEAN ACCIDENT AND GUARANTEE CORPORATION, LIMITED.   (See page 2.)

THE DAILY GRAPHIC

ONE PENNY

CORONATION EDITION.   LONDON : FRIDAY, JUNE 23, 1911.   **CORONATION EDITION.**

No. 6720 —Vol. LXXXVI.

CROWNED!

HIS MOST GRACIOUS MAJESTY KING GEORGE V., WEARING ST. EDWARD'S CROWN, RETURNING TO
BUCKINGHAM PALACE AFTER HIS CORONATION.

20 PAGES.

DAILY SKETCH

No. 715.—MONDAY, JUNE 26, 1911. THE PREMIER PICTURE PAPER. [Registered as a Newspaper.] ONE HALFPENNY.

THE KING AND QUEEN AFTER THE CORONATION.

Their Majesties photographed at Buckingham Palace immediately after returning from the Coronation ceremony at Westminster Abbey.
Photograph by W. and D. Downey.

THE DAILY MIRROR, Tuesday, June 20, 1911.

QUEEN MARY SPECIAL NUMBER.

The Daily Mirror

THE MORNING JOURNAL WITH THE SECOND LARGEST NET SALE

No. 2,387.	Registered at the G.P.O. as a Newspaper.	TUESDAY, JUNE 20, 1911	One Halfpenny.

QUEEN MARY AS A MOTHER: HER MAJESTY PHOTOGRAPHED WITH FOUR OF HER CHILDREN.

A trait in the Queen's character which has specially endeared her to her subjects is her love of home life and children. Her Majesty has six children, five boys and one girl. Formerly she used to give one day a week wholly to the children, but this rule has had to be modified lately according to existing circumstances. They have all been trained to love manly sports, the Queen herself teaching them to trundle hoops as a preliminary, and running races with them when they were quite little. Above, her Majesty is nursing Prince John, her youngest child. The other figures are Prince George, Princess Mary and Prince Henry.—(Sorrell.)

The Daily Mirror

THE MORNING JOURNAL WITH THE SECOND LARGEST NET SALE

No. 2,554.   Registered at the G.P.O as a Newspaper.   MONDAY, JANUARY 1, 1912   One Halfpenny.

THEIR MAJESTIES APPEAR BEFORE THEIR INDIAN SUBJECTS AT THE STATE GARDEN PARTY AT DELHI.

On the day following the unforgettable Durbar, the King-Emperor and Queen-Empress held a garden-party amid the exquisite marble buildings of Shah Jehan's Palace, in the Fort at Delhi, and afterwards showed themselves to the dense crowds gathered on the flats below The people were wild with delight, and shouted and cheered at the top of their voices. The photograph was taken while their Majesties were on the terrace of the Musammam Burj, the octagonal tower from which the Moghal Emperors used daily to show themselves.—(*Daily Mirror* photograph. By our Special Staff Photographer accompanying his Majesty.)

ROYAL WEDDING SPECIAL NUMBER.

The Daily Mirror

24 Pages

THE MORNING JOURNAL WITH THE SECOND LARGEST NET SALE.

No. 3,114. | Registered at the G.P.O. as a Newspaper. | THURSDAY, OCTOBER 16, 1913 | One Halfpenny.

THE ROYAL WEDDING SMILE: THE HAPPY PAIR LEAVE FOR THE HONEYMOON WITH A GOOD LUCK SHOE TIED TO THE MOTOR-CAR.

LN-6343

A laughing group, including the King and Queen, stood at the doorway of the Princess Royal's residence in Portman-square yesterday to bid good-bye to Prince Arthur of Connaught and the Duchess of Fife as they set off on their honeymoon. The large photograph shows the scene as the motor-car was about to leave. The King, wreathed in smiles, is standing next Princess Louise, Duchess of Argyll, while Princess May of Teck, one of the little bridesmaids, is laughing delightedly. Her Majesty is seen on the steps. Tied to the car is a lady's white shoe, the presence of which was probably not suspected by the occupants. The small picture shows the bride and bridegroom, who looked radiantly happy, standing on the balcony acknowledging the tumult of cheers from the throng below.

HUN GENERAL ARRESTED FOR 1914 OFFENCE

The Daily Mirror

CERTIFIED CIRCULATION LARGER THAN THAT OF ANY OTHER DAILY PICTURE PAPER

No. 4,723. | Registered at the G.P.O. as a Newspaper. | FRIDAY, DECEMBER 13, 1918 | [16 PAGES.] | One Penny.

THE KING'S VISIT TO THE FIELD OF GLORY AND SACRIFICE

The King in an American cemetery near the St. Quentin Canal.

The King inspects men of the Scottish Horse on the scene of some of their great achievements.

His Majesty amused by Hun dog which transferred allegiance to a British master.

A pause beside the lonely grave of three heroes of the Tank Corps.

The King was deeply affected as he traversed the ground on which the British armies won the splendid victories that were so potent a factor in bringing the war to a trium- phant close, and as he passed by the thickly-clustered crosses that mark the resting-places of the heroes who gave their lives that right might prevail.—(Official photographs)

VEDRINES' DARING FEAT: LANDS ON ROOF

The Daily Mirror

CERTIFIED CIRCULATION LARGER THAN THAT OF ANY OTHER DAILY PICTURE PAPER

No. 4,753. | Registered at the G.P.O. as a Newspaper. | MONDAY, JANUARY 20, 1919 | [16 PAGES.] | One Penny.

DEATH OF YOUNGEST SON OF KING AND QUEEN

Prince John on one of his earliest mounts.

Out for a spin on his bicycle.

Driving his own motor-car at Sandringham.

One of the most successful portraits of the Prince

Enjoying a visit to the London Zoological Gardens.

It is with the deepest regret that *The Daily Mirror* announces the death of Prince John, the King and Queen's youngest son. The Prince, who was thirteen years of age, had been in delicate health for some time, and had been living in retirement at Sandringham, where, on Saturday, he passed away.

LATE NIGHT SPECIAL.

Evening Standard

No. 30,449.   LONDON, TUESDAY,   FEB. 28, 1922.   ONE PENNY.

PRINCESS MARY'S HAPPY DAY

BRILLIANT SCENES AT THE ROYAL WEDDING.

Gigantic Crowds Cheer Princess and Her Husband.

LONDON ECHOES TO JOY BELLS.

Abbey Ceremony and Street Pageants Specially Described.

Princess Mary, only daughter of the King and Queen, to-day became the wife of Viscount Lascelles, K.G., D.S.O.

Nothing lacked to complete the appeal of a marriage which has caught the imagination of Britons all over the Empire: not even a Royal bride could have been favoured with brighter sunshine, and rarely has public enthusiasm been so completely reflected in the crowds about the streets.

Many of the scores and scores of thousands who assembled to cheer the Royal bride and her war-hero husband had taken up their positions as early as midnight. When the King's daughter appeared— the very picture of a bridal Princess—their fervid cheering was proof that even that long vigil had been well repaid.

After the ceremony the whole of London rang to the music of the pealing and "firing" of countless church bells.

In adjoining columns we publish a special account by Sir John Foster Fraser of the scene and the marriage ceremony in the Abbey.

CHEERED FROM PALACE TO ABBEY.

TUMULTUOUS WELCOME FOR THE KING AND THE BRIDE: VISION OF LOVELINESS: WOMEN SPECTATORS IN TEARS: THROUGH AVENUE OF ENTHUSIASM.

By Our Special Representatives.

The scene outside Buckingham Palace was one of memorable character. Enormous crowds had gathered from the early hours of the morning.

Those who were able to see certainly had one of the best positions on the route, for there was constant movement. The passing of the Guards, the turn-out of the Royal Scots, the playing of music, and the journeying to and fro of motors and State coaches enabled the crowd to while away in an interesting manner a long wait before the beginning of the procession.

Immediately outside the main gates were between 600 and 700 ticket holders who were accommodated on the broad pathways fronting the Victoria Memorial. These include nurses, girl guides, and representatives of various notable schools.

Wounded and disabled soldiers, brought from various hospitals in the London district, were given places on the north side of the Victoria Gardens, where they would obtain a view of both the outward and return processions.

It was at three minutes past eleven that the Queen, the Duke of York, Prince Henry, and Prince George came out. There was a great roar of cheering that succeeded the playing of the National Anthem, and her Majesty bowed smilingly in acknowledgment.

Less than a quarter of an hour later the great event of the morning took place. Princess Mary set out for the wedding ceremony.

The King and the bride emerged from the Grand Hall a couple of minutes before 11.15, and at once entered the waiting coach, that known as the Irish Coach.

The King was wearing the uniform of the Grenadier Guards out of compliment to the bridegroom. He handed his daughter into the carriage, and she took her place on the further side of the seat, so that when the King had joined her she was seated on her father's right hand.

The Princess was a perfect vision of loveliness in her magnificent wedding dress, her bridal veil and orange blossom. She was exceedingly pale.

As the carriage passed out of the quadrangle

(Continued on Page Eight.)

BRIDAL SCENE.

Impressive Grandeur of a Gracious Ceremony.

PICTURE IN THE ABBEY.

By SIR JOHN FOSTER FRASER.

In a shimmer of silver and lace, Princess Mary, the only daughter of the King, has been given in wedlock to Viscount Lascelles.

The precious old Abbey of Westminster, hallowed by a thousand years, has witnessed many memorable scenes, but none more affectingly beautiful than this, when a fair young English Princess and a gallant English soldier plighted their troth before the Almighty and in the presence of a great congregation of their countrypeople.

As the Princess, with no veil shielding her pale face, and resting on the arm of the King, came up the noble nave, flanked by the picturesque Yeomen of the Guard, and the choir sang "Lead us, Heavenly Father," and all men bowed and all women curtsied, the spectacle was one of impressive grandeur.

For all that was great and worthy

Sir VICTOR MACKENZIE.

ANTHEM AT THE PALACE.

The second of to-day's incidents occurred outside Buckingham Palace.

When the Royal processions had returned spectators massed in ever-growing numbers before the gates, all eyes turned to the main balcony.

Presently Princess Mary appeared in her bridal attire, with Viscount Lascelles. As the cheers grew in volume the King and Queen and Queen Alexandra came to the window.

Someone started to sing "God Save the King," and a moment later the whole vast assembly had joined in a mighty rendering of the National Anthem.

and representative in England had gathered to witness the ceremony. The Queen, accompanied by three of her sons—the Duke of York, Prince Henry and Prince George—had come earlier. Near by was the

beloved Queen Alexandra and her daughter, the Princess Victoria.

His Grace of Canterbury, heavily robed, the Lord Archbishop of York, the Bishop of London, and other high ecclesiastical dignitaries were assembled. Members of Lords and Commons and their ladies were there, my Lord Chancellor, the Prime Minister, the Speaker.

Whilst the great organ was pealing forth Sir Hubert Parry's "Bridal March" there quietly entered from a door in the Poet's Corner Lord Lascelles, the bridegroom, soldier-garbed, accompanied by his grooms-

THE BRIDE AT THE CENOTAPH.

Two incidents in particular will remain vividly impressed on the memory of all beholders.

The first was when the Royal bridal couple, now husband and wife, passed back again from the Abbey up Whitehall.

At the Cenotaph they stopped, she the radiant bride, he the gallant soldier.

Part of the bridal bouquet was passed through the carriage window and laid with the wreaths at the base of the column.

For a moment even the cheering was hushed. Then it broke out again. . . But many of the spectators' voices were now broken with tears.

man, Major Sir Victor Mackenzie, and he took his seat by the steps leading to the Sanctuary, awaiting the coming of his Royal bride.

Picture then the setting for the gracious ceremony.

A soft light illuminated the noble church. The organ was throbbing with gladsome music.

Everyone was in wedding costume—a radiance of beautiful gowns and Court attire and the full dress of regiments and ships. There was the flash of rare stones and a gentle aroma, not of incense, but of delicate perfumery, bringing the languor of flowers into the saintly Abbey.

THE KING AND THE BRIDE.

The two Queens had come with their Lord Chamberlains and Mistresses of the Robes. There were those akin in blood to their Majesties gathered round. Then came the King with his daughter, and following were the sweet girl bridesmaids.

A little smile accompanied the short upward glance of Princess Mary as her lover stepped by her side. And how exquisitely the music soared!

So bride and bridegroom stood before the altar in the presence of the Prelates of the

On the balcony at the Palace—the King, Princess Mary and Viscount Lascelles, Queen Alexandra, and the Queen responding to the ovation from the crowd.

ALPS CROSSED IN 1,000 MILE FLIGHT

with "Daily Mirror" Pictures: See Page 3

The Daily Mirror

NET SALE MUCH THE LARGEST OF ANY DAILY PICTURE NEWSPAPER

24 PAGES

No. 6,087. | Registered at the G.P.O. as a Newspaper. | WEDNESDAY, MAY 9, 1923 | One Penny.

THE KING AND QUEEN IN ROME

Special Pictures Brought to London in Thrilling Aeroplane Dash Across Europe

The Queen, with Queen Elena, driving from the gaily decked station at Rome to the Quirinal on the arrival of the King and Queen on their state visit to the King and Queen of Italy. The scene was one of remarkable enthusiasm, bright sunshine making the spectacle brilliant in the extreme. The Queen wore a magnificent gown of blue and silver which reflected the sun's rays in dazzling splendour, while the gay uniforms of the escort and the trappings of their horses shone in the clear daylight. The streets were filled with eager crowds of all classes, who waved and shouted a fervid welcome to the royal guests. This picture, with that on page 24, was brought to London by air in a thrilling express flight across Europe by the well-known airman Mr. A. J. Cobham.—(" Daily Mirror" photograph.)

SUZANNE'S OWN STORY OF "WONDERFUL WIMBLEDON"

DAILY SKETCH

No. 5,367. Telephones {London—Museum **9841.** Manchester—City **6501.**

LONDON, TUESDAY, JUNE 22, 1926. [Registered as a Newspaper.] ONE PENNY.

THE KING'S HANDSHAKE FOR SUZANNE

The King shaking hands with Mlle. Suzanne Lenglen yesterday at the opening of Wimbledon's jubilee fortnight of lawn tennis. He was accompanied by the Queen, who presented jubilee commemoration medals to winners of the various championships since the inception of the All-England Club.—(Daily Sketch.)

Mrs. Godfree (Kitty McKane) making obeisance to the Queen. She was champion in 1924.—(Daily Sketch.)

H. W. Austin, the brilliant young Cambridge player (left), in play against B. R. Lawrence, whom he defeated in the first round of the gentlemen's singles. Lord Cholmondeley (second from left) was also victorious, his victim being F. Bryans. France suffered a reverse in the defeat of P. Feret by Baron de Kehrling, the Hungarian star (right). The other picture shows Mlle. Lenglen dealing with a high return in the exhibition match in which she partnered Miss Ryan against Mrs. Godfree and Miss Bouman.—(Daily Sketch.)

THE DAILY MIRROR, Wednesday, August 29, 1934.

Broadcasting · Page 20

Daily Mirror

THE DAILY PICTURE NEWSPAPER WITH THE LARGEST NET SALE

PEER IN LIFEBOAT RESCUE

No. 9,596	Registered at the G.P.O. as a Newspaper.	WEDNESDAY, AUGUST 29, 1934	One Penny

PRINCE GEORGE ENGAGED

Betrothal to Princess Marina of Greece

THE KING GIVES HIS "GLAD CONSENT" BY WIRE

Surprise Holiday Romance

Prince George, the fourth and youngest son of King George and Queen Mary, is engaged to Princess Marina of Greece.

THE announcement, which will be received with pleasure throughout the land, was made in the Court Circular last night in the following terms:

Balmoral Castle,
August 28.

"It is with the greatest pleasure that the King and Queen announce the betrothal of their dearly beloved son the Prince George to the Princess Marina, daughter of the Prince and Princess Nicolas of Greece, to which union the King has gladly given his consent."

The engagement, which has come as a delightful surprise even to the Court, is the culmination of a holiday romance.

Prince George met his future bride in London five years ago, when she was paying a private visit to this country.

From time to time they met on her succeeding visits, and it was known that they had become close friends.

On August 15, Prince George went by air to Yugoslavia to be the guest of Prince Paul (Princess Marina's brother-in-law) at his summer residence on Bohinisko Lake.

In a week, amid the romantic surroundings of the Slovenian Alps, the friendship of the Royal pair ripened into love.

Prince George proposed to the Princess, and was accepted.

He at once wired to Balmoral Castle for the King's consent.

The King replied by wire with his "glad consent."

The Royal lovers have also received the consent of Princess Marina's parents.

An Outdoor Girl

The *Daily Mirror* understands that no plans whatever have yet been made regarding the marriage.

Before it can take place the King must give his formal consent by an Order in Council, under the terms of the Royal Personages Marriage Act.

Prince George, as one of the King's children, receives an annual grant under the Civil List. With the exception of the Prince of Wales, the sons of the King were granted by Act of Parliament in 1910 annuities of £10,000 each on attaining majority, to be increased by a further £15,000 each on marriage.

Princess Marina, who is a tall, charming brunette will celebrate her twenty-eighth birthday on November 30. She was born in Athens in 1906, and is the youngest of the three daughters of Prince Nicolas of Greece. She dances and shoots—two amusements of which Prince George is very fond.

One who knows her well said in London last night: "She is a typical modern girl, very fond of outdoor sport."

(Continued on page 3)

Princess Marina of Greece and Prince George of England, who it was announced last night have become engaged. The Princess is daughter of Prince and Princess Nicolas of Greece. See also back page.

THE THANKSGIVING SERVICE, by Lady Oxford

WIRELESS: P. 35

DAILY SKETCH

Pages of JUBILEE PICTURES

No. 8,120   [Registered as a newspaper.]   TUESDAY, MAY 7, 1935   ONE PENNY

AND SO SAY ALL OF US!

The King's appearance on the balcony of Buckingham Palace after the return from St. Paul's was hailed by a crowd of 100,000 with scenes of wild enthusiasm. After singing the National Anthem and cheering unceasingly for several minutes, the great gathering burst spontaneously into the singing of "For He's a Jolly Good Fellow." As the strains of the old song reached the King's ears this photograph was taken. It shows his obvious delight at his people's affectionate tribute. With him in the picture are Princess Margaret Rose, the Hon. Gerald Lascelles, the Earl of Harewood and Princess Elizabeth raising her white-gloved hand in salute. Another wonderful picture of the balcony scene appears on pages 18 and 23.

HEART TO HEART AT THE ZOO, by HUBERT S. BANNER

WIRELESS: P. 20

DAILY SKETCH

No. 8,122   [Registered as a newspaper.]   THURSDAY, MAY 9, 1935   ONE PENNY

CHILDREN'S GREAT DAY
Jubilee Celebrated With Tea Parties and Fun

BUSY TIMES FOR THE QUEEN

In spite of her many Jubilee engagements the Queen found time for a little afternoon shopping yesterday. Here, she is leaving a shop off Brompton-road.

Yesterday was an important Jubilee occasion for the children. In the top picture the Rev. W. Smith, in a Union Jack hat, is sharing their enjoyment of the Jubilee tea party given in Harrison-street, King's Cross. Below is the Mayor of Hastings with two of his 7,000 young guests at an entertainment in Alexandra Park, Hastings.

Evening Standard

No. 34,696 LONDON, WEDNESDAY, NOVEMBER 6, 1935 ONE PENNY

TO-DAY'S ROYAL BRIDE

THE DUKE OF GLOUCESTER

Big Crowd Cheer Lady Alice

A BRIGHT, SUNNY MORNING

THE Duke of Gloucester, third son of the King and Queen, was married at Buckingham Palace this morning to Lady Alice Montagu-Douglas-Scott, daughter of the late Duke of Buccleuch.

It was a sunny, crisp November day, and the bride was greeted by an enormous crowd as she drove down Constitution Hill

The Bride Leaves Five Minutes Earlier

"AS good a day as they could possibly have," was the experts' early forecast of the weather for the wedding of the Duke of Gloucester and Lady Alice Scott.

"The whole morning will be fine with good visibility and an average temperature. There will be no rain."

By a last-minute change in the arrangements it was decided that the Royal bride should leave her home in Grosvenor-place five minutes earlier, arriving at Buckingham Palace at 11.23 instead of 11.28.

The reason is to avoid any possible hitch in the wedding plans.

The day dawned bright and clear, though cold. This encouraged many sightseers from outlying suburbs to make an early journey to London, consoling themselves for the absence of an Abbey ceremony by the thought that they would be able to see the Royal couple drive from the Palace to St. Pancras in an open carriage in the afternoon.

In the Chapel

Shorn of public ceremonial because of the recent death of the bride's father, the Royal wedding remained an occasion of stateliness and dignity.

To mark his association with the Army, the Duke of Gloucester had chosen the blue, gold and red full-dress uniform of a major

of the 10th Royal Hussars for his wedding. The King decided to wear military uniform, that of a field-marshal.

The chapel—where the King and Queen make their devotions on Sundays—is hidden in the south-west wing of the Palace. Its windows are not visible from outside the Palace grounds.

To-day it was decorated with hundreds and hundreds of white flowers.

On the altar in two gold vases stood sheaves of longiflorum lilies flanking the Charles II. gold altar plate.

On either side of the altar stood two tall spires of white flowers—lilies, lilac and chrysanthemums.

The gilt communion rails with their crimson plush top were garlanded with festoons of lilies, white heather, orange blossom, tuber roses and narcissi.

Sheaves, six feet high, of lilies, white heather and chrysanthemums ornamented each of the six white pillars on either side of the chapel.

The whole of the chapel floral scheme was designed by Mr. Goodyear, the Court florist.

(Continued on PAGE FIVE)

IN HER WEDDING DRESS: a specially posed picture of Lady Alice Scott wearing the dress in which she was married.

INDEX

Daily Mirror

THE DAILY PICTURE NEWSPAPER WITH THE LARGEST NET SALE

EMPIRE IN MOURNING

No. 10,028 — Registered at the G.P.O. as a Newspaper. — TUESDAY, JANUARY 21, 1936 — One Penny

DEATH OF THE KING

The King in the uniform of Admiral of the Fleet—his Silver Jubilee portrait.

THE "Daily Mirror" announces with the deepest regret that his Majesty King George V died last night at Sandringham. He was aged seventy.

He had been ill only four days, but because of his serious illness in 1928 his attack of bronchial catarrh had caused the gravest anxiety.

The seriousness of his condition was revealed by the mention of heart weakness in the first bulletin issued on Friday night. Next day the doctors used the words, "cause for anxiety."

King George V had reigned for twenty-five years. It was only last May that the Empire joined in paying Silver Jubilee homage to a monarch who had guided his people through the difficult years of the Great War and the difficult years that followed.

Such sincere rejoicings were surely unique in history. King George, by his devotion to duty, his brave example in every crisis, had won the love of the greatest Empire of all.

The hearts of the citizens of that Empire will go out to the gracious Queen Mary and other members of the Royal Family in this great bereavement.

By the death of his father, the Prince of Wales now becomes the King-Emperor, and presumably will be known as King Edward VIII.

DAILY EXPRESS, Wednesday, January 22, 1936

Daily Express

TODAY'S WEATHER: FINE. RADIO PROGRAMME: PAGE 6.

No. 11,135 WEDNESDAY, JANUARY 22, 1936 ONE PENNY

LAST WORDS OF KING GEORGE WERE: "HOW IS THE EMPIRE?"

"All Is Well, Sire," Was The Reply

The King, Smiling, Passed Into His Last Sleep

FUNERAL AT WINDSOR ON TUESDAY

SIMULTANEOUSLY with the announcement that the funeral of King George the Fifth will take place at Windsor on Tuesday, the Prime Minister, Mr. Stanley Baldwin, revealed to the nation, over the radio last night, the King's last words.

In a brief interval of consciousness, Mr. Baldwin said, King George sent for his secretary, "How is the Empire?" King George asked. And the secretary said "All is well, Sire, with the Empire."

"At the words" said Mr. Baldwin "the King gave him a smile and relapsed once more into unconsciousness."

Mr. Baldwin began by saying: "Most of what passes near the end is sacred, and we none of us have desire or right to inquire into what happens at those times, yet I think I may tell you this.

"Each time the King became conscious it was some kind inquiry or kind observation of some one, some words of gratitude for kindness shown."

Mr. Baldwin then told of the King's last words, and said:—

"During all that time, sub-consciously and just coming to the surface at odd moments was that same love for his people, care for their well-being here and throughout the world, for that family to whom he spoke last Christmas. The thought of them was with him to the end.

"King George, it is true, inherited his position on the throne, but he won his own way to the hearts of the people. Behind the pomp and the pageantry incidental to his great position he laboured night and day in that high station to which God had called him.

"DOING HIS DUTY ENOBLED HIS CHARACTER"

"The doing of his duty to the utmost of his ability was the guiding principle of his life. Great power which corrupts weak natures ennobled our King's character and made him subdue passion and will and energy to his duty to his country.

"He brought the dispositions that are lovely in private life into service and the conduct of the Commonwealth, and, not only in virtue of his office, but in virtue of his person was he the First Gentleman in the Land.

"Every heart in the Empire is sore for Queen Mary this night. In a married life so perfect, so happy as theirs was, there has to come that inevitable day when one is taken and the other is left, and one of the two has to continue the pilgrimage to the end alone.

"There are millions of hands which, if they could reach the Queen, would be stretched out to her, and tears of sympathy to shed with her. It must be some

PAGE TWO, COLUMN SIX

MR. BALDWIN driving from the House of Commons after last night's meeting.

DEATHBED SERVICE

ARCHBISHOP READS SPECIAL PRAYERS

THE Court Circular last night made the following announcement:—

"SANDRINGHAM,
"21st January, 1936.

"The King passed peacefully away last evening at 11.55 o'clock.

"During the last moments of his Majesty the Archbishop of Canterbury read special prayers and conducted a short service in the King's room.

"This evening the coffin, escorted by a detachment of the King's Company, Grenadier Guards, and followed by the Queen and other members of the Royal Family, was taken to Sandringham Church, where a private service was held."

KING COMES BY AIR TO LONDON

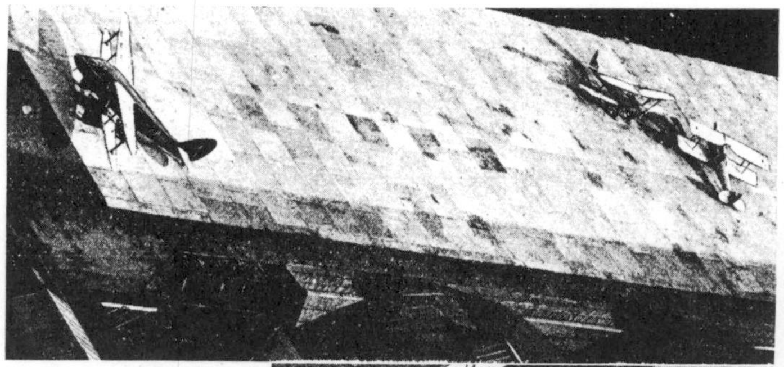

At Hendon King Edward's airpiane alighted after his flight, with the Duke of York, from Bircham Newton. Royal cars awaited them.—*Pictures taken from the "Daily Express" airplane.*

WHERE TO HEAR TODAY'S PROCLAMATION

The accession to the Throne of King Edward VIII. will be proclaimed throughout the Empire this morning.

This is the London programme:—

10 a.m.—Garter King of Arms proclaims the King at Friary-court, St. James's Palace. Proclamation guns fire salutes at Hyde Park and at Tower of London.

10.15 a.m. (approximately).—Lancaster Herald proclaims the King at Charing Cross.

10.30 a.m. (approximately).—Norroy King of Arms proclaims the King at Temple Bar.

10.45 a.m. (approximately).—Clarenceux King of Arms proclaims the King at the Royal Exchange.

LORDS AND COMMONS' FAREWELL TO THE KING

THE funeral of King George will take place at St. George's Chapel, Windsor, on Tuesday.

A special train, leaving Wolverton at noon tomorrow, will bring the King's body to Paddington. The Queen Mother and other members of the Royal Family will travel in the train. They will arrive at Paddington at 2.30.

Until the day of the funeral, the King will lie in state in Westminster Hall on a purple-draped catalfalque.

When the body arrives at Westminster Hall, Lords and Commons will be there assembled to receive King George V. for the last time.

In June, the M.P.s and peers stood in the same hall to listen to the King's speech as he returned thanks for addresses of congratulation on his Silver Jubilee.

The King's voice rang round the ancient hall. Then the Lord Chancellor, Lord Sankey, flinging aside form and ceremony called for three cheers for the King and Queen. Parliament cheered till the echoes shouted back.

Tomorrow there will be silence and mourning

The Lords, led by their Speaker, the Lord Chancellor, and the Commons by their's, Captain FitzRoy, are to march in slow procession from their Houses to Westminster Hall for the ceremony.

The Archbishop of Canterbury, assisted by the Chaplain of the House of Commons, will lead the hymns and prayers.

Soon it will be over.

The lying-in-state will last until Monday night. On Tuesday, Parliament will say farewell to King George, as his body is borne to Westminster Abbey, and thence to Windsor for burial.

King Edward and other members of the Royal Family may visit the Hall during the lyin-in-state,

King Edward Urged To Give Up Flying

KING EDWARD VIII. flew from Sandringham to his capital yesterday—the first British monarch ever to fly. Today, if flying weather permits, he will return to Sandringham by air.

Now those who are close to him are urging him in future to use airplanes only in cases of urgency.

They base their plea on two arguments: the safety of the King's person, and the tremendous responsibility placed on the shoulders of the man who pilots his airplane. They plead that this is more than one man should be asked to bear.

The King is a keen airman. It is likely that he will continue to use airplanes for long journeys.

He has told his friends he is convinced that the day is not far distant when airplanes will be used as freely as cars are used today.

There are probably not fifty people in the country with a longer flying record than the King's.

He made his first flight in 1913. at the age of nineteen, in an Army airship. Since then he has himself piloted nearly every type of aircraft.

AIR SERVICE IN WAR

On his Air Chief Marshal's tunic he wears the silver wings of an R.A.F. pilot.

He earned those wings in the open cockpits of R.A.F. fighters under R.A.F. instructors.

During the war he flew over the enemy lines.

When the first practical British light civil type airplanes arrived he was one of the first to use them. He has flown half across Europe and the English Channel in a day in an old single-engined open light airplane.

Later, he took to enclosed cabin machines as they appeared.

The encouragement of flying in Britain by personal example has been his creed. Now he has two private aircraft of his own.

F.A. CUP TIES —AS ARRANGED

OTHER GAMES OPTIONAL

All racing, Rugby Union, and greyhound racing fixtures have been cancelled till after Tuesday, the day of the funeral.

The Football Association decided that its members may carry out their fixtures if they so wish, except on Tuesday next.

All F.A. Cup fourth round ties due to be decided next Saturday will be played as arranged.

The Football League decided that all matches under their jurisdiction should be played.

A complete list of sports fixtures cancelled is on Page Sixteen.

LAVAL EXPECTED TO RESIGN TODAY

PRESIDENT FOR LONDON

"Daily Express" Correspondent.
PARIS, Tuesday.

M. Laval's Cabinet is generally expected to resign tomorrow after the Cabinet council.

Earlier in the day it was thought that in order to enable President Lebrun to attend the King's funeral, it would be necessary to postpone the Cabinet crisis.

But it is now believed that the new Government can be formed in time for M. Lebrun to attend the ceremony in London.

Duchess Of York Motors To London

The Duchess of York, who has been at Royal Lodge, Windsor, suffering from influenzial pneumonia since a week before Christmas, has made an excellent recovery and yesterday motored to London to her house in Piccadilly.

The Duke joined her there and today they will go to Sandringham. Their two children, Princess Elizabeth and Princess Margaret Rose are remaining at Royal Lodge, Windsor.

HOW THE KING ARRIVED

HIS CAR HELD UP

Only a handful of people saw King Edward VIII. and the Duke of York arrive at Hendon yesterday (writes a "Daily Express" representative.

The King stepped out of the airplane wearing a thick dark overcoat and a dark suit. His face looked pale and drawn.

With his brother he entered a waiting car and left for St. James's Palace.

No route had been cleared for the car. Twice it was compelled to stop in traffic hold-ups.

KAISER GRIEVES FOR HIS COUSIN

Cancels Plans For Birthday

"Daily Express" Special Correspondent.
DOORN, Tuesday.

OVER the little village of Doorn a flag flies at half-mast. Early today it conveyed the news to most of the villagers that a great and friendly King had died.

In the big mansion beneath the flag the death it signalises has caused deep grief. The ex-Kaiser is mourning the loss of his favourite cousin.

He has cancelled or altered all his engagements, and is deeply moved by the sad death of his kinsman. He is receiving no visitors for the moment, and is keeping indoors.

"I Am Deeply Affected"

This is the telegram which he sent to Queen Mary:—

"I am deeply affected by the tragic loss you and the Royal Family have to deplore. I beg you to accept the warmest sympathy of Hermine, myself and all the members of my house.

"(Signed) WILHELM."

An official of the Court told me today:—

"The Kaiser had a great affection for his cousin. Before the war they saw a good deal of each other, and the Kaiser always had a great admiration for the fine character of the King.

"He had planned to give enjoyment to many people in the celebration of his own seventy-sixth birthday which falls next Monday, but the news of King George's death caused him immediately to cancel all arrangements, and the birthday will now be merely an ordinary family reunion. Nobody from outside the family will be invited.

Crown Prince May Be At Funeral

"At the funeral of the King the Kaiser will be represented by one of his sons, probably the Crown Prince, but he has not definitely made his final choice.

"Since the moment when he first heard that the King was ill he commanded me to keep him informed of every development as reported by the doctors and as obtained from personal sources.

"Ever since the King's illness became serious the Kaiser has spoken of his friendship with his cousin in the years when they used to see each other either in England or in Germany.

"I know that the news I bore to him last night has saddened him more than anything else for years."

LATEST NEWS

Telephone: Central 8000

IN MY FATHER'S FOOTSTEPS

—THE KING

Making declaration at Privy Council meeting the King said:

"I am determined to follow in my father's footsteps and to work as he did throughout his life for the happiness and welfare of all classes of my subjects."

King Edward leaving Sandringham yesterday with his brother and heir, the Duke of York, for Bircham Newton Airdrome.

St. IVEL EASILY DIGESTED

CHEESE

2/6 8½

Aplin & Barrett Limited, Yeovil, Somerset.

Evening Standard

LATE NIGHT FINAL

To-morrow's Weather—
Unsettled; Mild

Lighting-up Time
To-day, 5.9 p.m.

Memorial
Number:

TEN PAGES
OF PICTURES

No. 34,765   LONDON, TUESDAY, JANUARY 28, 1936   ONE PENNY

HOME TO WINDSOR

HIS LAST RESTING-PLACE: The coffin of King George approaching the entrance to Windsor Castle this afternoon.

CHAPTER 3

EDWARD VIII

*The public were blissfully
unaware of the drama that was to come.*

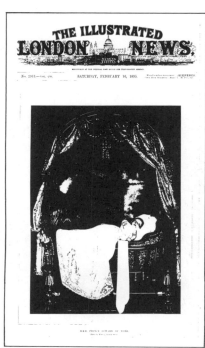

The romance of King Edward VIII and the American divorcee Wallis Simpson was not just one of the great newspaper stories of the century. It was a story in which the conduct of the newspapers themselves earned a lasting and controversial place in British history.

Continental and American newspapers were printing suggestive reports about the King's friendship with Mrs Simpson long before the British public had even heard of her. The strength of Edward's feelings were of course known in high places, but the British press — led by two of its most powerful proprietors, Lord Beaverbrook of the *Daily Express* and Lord Rothermere of the *Daily Mail* — agreed to enter upon what has been called "a conspiracy of silence".

Edward's reign began, at least, in happy and glorious style. The thoughtful young monarch appeared a rather poignant figure on the front pages which greeted his accession — the *Evening Standard* (p.38) noting that by flying to London from Sandringham on his father's death, he became the first British monarch to travel by air.

The customary good omens for the reign were ritually rehearsed — and there was still the King's little nieces, the Princesses Elizabeth and Margaret, to add to the delight of picture editors (p.68). Despite the economic austerity of the 1930s, Britain sensed the possibility of a bright new era under one of the world's most appealing and seemingly approachable monarchs.

So there was national outrage in the summer when an apparently deranged man rushed at him on Constitution Hill, brandishing a revolver. The *Daily Sketch* thought the incident worth six pages of photographs.

As late as November 1936, when Edward was already privately weighing the agonies of abdication, the public was blissfully unaware as it applauded his visit to unemployed miners in South Wales (p.39) — immortalised by his famous phrase "Something must be done." Here was a King, it seemed, who would use his position to appeal to the consciences of politicians.

But his first meeting with Beaverbrook had taken place over a month before, when the King pleaded with the newspaper tycoon to play down coverage of Mrs Simpson's divorce proceedings. "The Beaver" did not yet realise that Edward planned to marry Wallis Simpson — but he sensed the dangers to the Crown of a scandal. With Rothermere, who was also chairman of the Newspaper Proprietors Association, he got other papers

to agree to "a policy of discretion". The British press reported the divorce case with due restraint, and no innuendo — unlike America's, where one newspaper came up with the immortal headline: KING'S MOLL RENO'D IN WOLSEY'S HOME TOWN.

Over that month there was much coming and going between the monarch, the Prime Minister (Stanely Baldwin), the Archbishop of Canterbury and the press barons. But British newspapers maintained their silence, even when *The New York Journal* printed an article headlined: KING WILL WED WALLY.

The one national editor constantly threatening to break ranks was Geoffrey Dawson of *The Times*. Dawson told the Cabinet Secretary that "*The Times* will have to do something about the King and Mrs Simpson, but the PM must tell me what he wants done." Baldwin told Dawson that he wanted nothing done. But on the morning of December 1 the Bishop of Bradford, Dr A. W. F. Blunt, delivered himself of a sermon about the religious nature of the forthcoming coronation service — taken by the provincial press as code words for his disapproval of the King's private life. The dam had burst, and the matter was next morning laid before the nation.

The drama was over within ten days: Edward abdicated on December 10. His famous speech of departure was dramatically printed in its entirety on the front page of the *Evening Standard* (p.44), as was indeed the due of this unprecedented Royal drama.

But the public was deeply angry that the whole debate had taken place behind their backs, as witnessed by the famous *Daily Mirror* front page, listing the five things 45,000,000 PEOPLE DEMAND TO KNOW (p.41). They also suspected, not without some reason, plots by politicians and press lords against their King.

Public opinion questioned the need for the King to renounce his throne — and afterwards for Edward and his bride to live in exile. All through the rest of his long life, the Duke of Windsor remained an object of fascination to his former subjects, and one to whom an increasingly sympathetic attitude was taken.

Elizabeth II, sensing the public mood, took careful steps to show greater courtesy to both Duke and Duchess than her parents had felt possible. When at last the Duke died in 1972 (p.46), one of the most poignant press photos of recent years showed his widow peeping through the lace curtains of Buckingham Palace — whose doors had for so long been barred to her.

FIVE PAGES OF PICTURES ILLUSTRATING THE NATIONAL TRAGEDY.

THE DAILY GRAPHIC

ONE PENNY

LONDON : MONDAY, MAY 9, 1910.

No. 6368.—Vol. LXXXII.

Registered as a Newspaper.

THE NEW REIGN.

HIS MAJESTY KING GEORGE V., WITH HIS ELDEST SON, PRINCE EDWARD, HEIR TO THE THRONE.

("Daily Graphic" photograph.)

The Daily Mirror

THE MORNING JOURNAL WITH THE SECOND LARGEST NET SALE

No. 2,407.   Registered at the G.P.O. as a Newspaper.   THURSDAY, JULY 13, 1911   One Halfpenny.

HIS ROYAL HIGHNESS THE PRINCE OF WALES, WHOSE INVESTITURE TAKES PLACE AT CARNARVON CASTLE TO-DAY.

To-day the historic and picturesque Castle at Carnarvon will be the scene of the investiture and presentation of the Prince of Wales. The imagination of the Welsh people has been deeply stirred by the prospect of the wonderful pageant which is to be enacted amid such historic surroundings, and intense gratification is expressed at what is regarded as a special concession to the national feeling.

(1) A hitherto unpublished photograph of the Prince, taken thirteen years ago. It shows him with rifle and bluejacket's belt and bayonet. (2) Taken on board H.M.S. Crescent in 1898. (3) In ordinary attire. (4) In the robes he wore at the Coronation. He is dressed as a Knight of the Garter and is wearing a coronet.—(Cribb, Downey and Campbell Gray.)

The Daily Mirror

THE MORNING JOURNAL WITH THE SECOND LARGEST NET SALE

No. 2,408.   Registered at the G.P.O. as a Newspaper.   FRIDAY, JULY 14, 1911   One Halfpenny.

WALES RAPTUROUSLY ACCLAIMS HER PRINCE WHEN HE IS PRESENTED TO THE PEOPLE AFTER YESTERDAY'S INVESTITURE AT CARNARVON CASTLE.

With the grey walls of Carnarvon's historic and picturesque castle as a background, the Prince of Wales was invested and presented to the people by his father, the King, yesterday. Never was a site more suited for a pageant, and the beautiful and impressive scenes will never fade from the memory of those who were privileged to behold them. The ceremony was made the occasion of a remarkable display of loyal feeling by the Welsh people, who acclaimed their young Prince with no uncertain voice. Above, the Prince is seen being presented by his Majesty at the King's Gate.—(*Daily Mirror* photograph.)

DAILY SKETCH

No. 4,137. Telephones {London—Holborn 6510. Manchester—City 6501.   LONDON, WEDNESDAY, JUNE 21, 1922. [Registered as a Newspaper.] ONE PENNY.

OUR PRINCE'S HOMECOMING.

The Prince's response was as hearty as the welcome that was given him.

The Prince on the Renown, which has been his home during a large part of the tour.—(Daily Sketch.)

The Duke of York, who went on board the Renown to welcome his brother home. With him in the photograph is Miss Edwina Ashley, whose engagement to Lord Louis Mountbatten, the Prince's cousin and naval Aide-de-Camp, was a romance of the tour.

There were glad and memorable scenes on the battleship Renown as she returned once more to British waters. To-day London will receive the Prince with the gratitude that the success of his great mission has earned and with the joy that his popularity inspires.

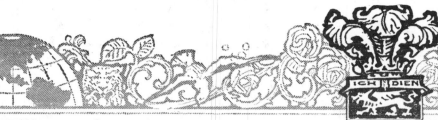

H.M.S. RENOWN

36

"VIRGIN OF THE FOREST": *New Serial on Page 16*

DAILY SKETCH
INCORPORATING THE DAILY GRAPHIC

No. 6,836.   [Registered as a newspaper.]   TUESDAY, MARCH 17, 1931.   ONE PENNY.

CONTROL MARRIAGE *By* Lord DONEGALL

THE PRINCE: PICTURES BY AIR FROM BUENOS AIRES

The Prince surrounded by an enthusiastic crowd as he entered his car for the British Embassy.

Descending from his aeroplane on arrival at Mar del Plata.

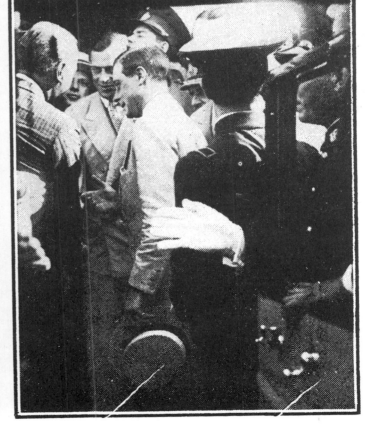

At the British Embassy with President Uriburu and the British Ambassador, Sir Ronald Macleay.

The Prince and Prince George entering their car at Retiro Station.

Above are the first pictures of the Prince of Wales's arrival at Buenos Aires, the capital of the Argentine, to be brought to England. Aeropostale (the French mail organisation) left Buenos Aires with them at midnight, March 6, for Natal, Brazil. From there they were conveyed by fast steamer to Dakar, West Africa, and brought to London, via Toulouse, by aeroplane. The Prince opened the British Trade Exhibition at Buenos Aires on Saturday.

Evening Standard

To-morrow's Weather—
Cold, Showers.

Lighting-up Time
To-day 4.56 p.m.

No. 34,759   LONDON, TUESDAY, JANUARY 21, 1936   ONE PENNY

NEW KING'S JOURNEY
Edward VIII. Comes to London by Air

ACCESSION COUNCIL AND PARLIAMENT MEETING TO-DAY

COURT MOURNING FOR NINE MONTHS

KING EDWARD VIII. left Sandringham by car with the Duke of York to-day, drove to Bircham Newton R.A.F. Airdrome, and flew with his brother to Hendon. From Hendon he drove to St. James's Palace.

King Edward was thus the first King of England to travel by air.

A large crowd waited in the neighbourhood of St. James's Palace to welcome him. The people greeted the King with bared heads silently.

IN LONDON THIS AFTERNOON THE KING IS ATTENDING THE ACCESSION MEETING OF THE PRIVY COUNCIL. THIS IS BEING HELD AT ST. JAMES'S PALACE. IT WILL APPROVE A PROCLAMATION PROCLAIMING THE NEW KING. KING EDWARD WILL ADDRESS THE COUNCIL AND THE PRIVY COUNCILLORS WILL BE RE-SWORN.

THE PROCLAMATION OF KING EDWARD WILL TAKE PLACE AT 10 O'CLOCK TO-MORROW MORNING AT ST. JAMES'S PALACE, CHARING CROSS, TEMPLE BAR AND THE ROYAL EXCHANGE.

Parliament is meeting this evening and again to-morrow for the taking of the oath of allegiance to the new King.

On Thursday the Prime Minister will present a message to the Commons from the King. Both Houses will pass two motions—an address to the King and an address to Queen Mary.

King Edward visited Buckingham Palace this afternoon. According to present arrangements, he will return to Sandringham to-morrow.

MESSAGES OF SYMPATHY

FROM all parts of the world to-day came messages of sympathy.

In response to the King's message last night to the Lord Mayor of London the following reply was sent to Sandringham by the Lord Mayor:

I tender to your Royal Highness the deep sympathy and respectful condolence of the citizens of London in the sad loss which you and the members of the Royal Family have sustained.

His Majesty's memory and the record of his work and glorious reign will ever be dear to the hearts of my fellow citizens.

The heads of the fighting Services all sent expressions of their sympathy and loyalty.

COURT MOURNING

THE following notice was issued to-day from Buckingham Palace:

The King commands that the Court shall wear mourning for nine months from this day for his late most gracious Majesty King George V. of blessed memory.

The Court to change to half mourning on Tuesday, July 21 next, and on Wednesday, October 21 next, the Court to go out of mourning.

PLANS FOR THE FUNERAL

KING EDWARD has brought from Sandringham draft plans for the funeral arrangements made by himself in consultation with the Duke of York and Lord Wigram in the early hours of this morning.

The plans are being discussed to-night at a conference at York House with the Duke of Norfolk, the Earl Marshal, and heads of the forces and others.

(CONTINUED ON PAGE TWO)

KING EDWARD VIII.

King George and King Edward

A SECTION of biographical studies contributed to the "Evening Standard" by famous writers begins on Page Seven. The contributors include

The Very Rev. W. R. INGE, D.D.   SIR GEORGE ARTHUR

JOHN DRINKWATER   R. H. BRUCE LOCKHART

COURT OF ALDERMEN MEET—PAGE THREE.
TO-DAY AT SANDRINGHAM AND WINDSOR—PAGE FIVE.
MEMORIAL SERVICE IN ST. PAUL'S—PAGE TWO.
SPORTS EVENTS CANCELLED—BACK PAGE.

South Wales Echo & Evening Express

SEVENTH EDITION

No. 16,513 Estab. 52 Years. ONE PENNY.

WEDNESDAY, NOVEMBER 18, 1936

THE KING'S DELIGHT AT SOUTH WALES RECEPTION

"Never Seen Such Enthusiasm" :: Equerry's Statement To "Echo"

SUNSHINE TOUR OF THE DARK AREAS

This was the first Royal occasion for a little maiden from Pontypridd, and she bought a flag to celebrate it.

Page of Pictures of the Royal Visit on Page 10

Miner-Farmers' Archway of Leeks :: "Send Me Some" Request

DINNER-TIME JOKE

"Any Complaints?"—Army Note at Pentrebach

"His Majesty is delighted with his reception in South Wales. The populace has rallied wonderfully for the occasion. I have never seen such enthusiasm."

This was the King's message, through his Equerry, after his triumphal first-day tour of some of the Special Areas in South Wales to-day.

Royal weather—blue skies, strong sunshine—and a right Royal greeting from his South Wales subjects marked the King's progress to-day when his Majesty started his tour.

It was a happy omen, this bright November day, indicative of South Wales's hopes of a nation's emergence from the shadows that have too long beset her.

Many and novel were the ways in which the Principality expressed her loyalty. Thus at Boverton, where his Majesty started his tour by visiting the Welsh Land Settlement Society's farm, unemployed miners turned land settlers, the King passed under an archway of leeks.

The King smilingly examined the construction of the leek arch and commented to the farm manager, Mr. Bean: "You can arrange to send some of these to London for me. I am fond of them."

The King spoke to many of the men and held a long conversation with a man named J. Dalton, a former Irish Guardsman, who told the King that he had waited on him on two occasions in France.

TRAGEDY

Rhondda Woman's Collapse

Tragedy attended the visit of the King to-day. Mrs. E. Jones, 120, Ynyscynon-road, Trealaw, aged 75, was one of the spectators on the route between Penygraig and Dinas. She was standing near the post office in Dinas when someone shouted, "Here is the King." She was noticed to collapse immediately afterwards, and was carried by willing helpers into the post office unconscious.

Dr. Watkins, Tonypandy, arrived in reply to a summons and found that Mrs. Jones had had a seizure. She was conveyed home in the ambulance van of the Porth and District Hospital, but died on her way there.

Mrs. Jones was well-known in religious circles in the Rhondda Valley, and had been caretaker at Dewi Sant Church, Tonypandy, for nearly 30 years.

The King inquired as to the wages he was receiving, and Dalton told him it was 30s. 6d. a week, but after deductions for rent he had £1 0s. 9½d. actually going into the house, out of which there were payments to be made of 3s. a week for coal, 2s. 6d. for electric light, and 2s. for family insurance.

Those Joneses!

The King commented: "It does not leave very much, does it?" Mr. Dalton answered, "No, sir, and very often we have to sit in the dark because we cannot afford the half-crown a week for the electric light."

The King asked another man the meaning of a badge he was wearing, on which was the number "36." The man explained that everyone at the farm wore numbers, which were really their numbers on the pay roll.

It is necessary, sir, for us to have numbers, as if you shouted out for Jones about 25 men would run towards you, and if you shouted out for Davies you would have over 30!"

The King laughed heartily and asked, "And which are you—Jones or Davies?"

"I am Albert Jones," answered the man.

In all, the King spoke to about 20 men. Of one he asked: "Do you like it better than mining?"

"No, I would rather be a miner, sir," answered the man, who came from Mardy, "but we are lucky indeed to have anything to do, and we always think of our pals at the Valleys, who are just sitting and looking at the empty mines."

"Yes, it is a great pity that something more can't be done about it," agreed the King.

Surprised Housewife

Characteristic of the King's homely charm was a visit to a cottager's dwelling. He surprised the housewife in the midst of her household duties and talked with her as though he were a neighbour dropped in for a chat.

"Happy?" Mrs. Newman, wife of a Gelligaer ex-miner, echoed the Royal visitor's question. "Yes—but, your Majesty, will you remember the others who are left in the Valleys?"

"Little Tich"

At Dinas, in the Rhondda, the King exchanged greetings with a still-crippled victim of the Ely pit cage crash of 1909, and with another man who boasted of 24 children.

To a nine-year-old ambulance cadet he smilingly said, "Little Tich is growing bigger."

His Majesty left Dinas to the full-throated singing of a huge crowd of "Hen Wlad fy Nhadau."

Pontypridd staged an exhibition of physical training by unemployed. "A wonderfully good display," was his Majesty's comment.

At Pentrebach the King was keenly interested in the intermediate training scheme, the only one of its kind in the country.

Any Complaints?

Before sitting down to his own luncheon he asked to see the dining-hall and the food being supplied to the men. He waited until they were all seated and, with typical humour, reminded many of them of their Army days. He stepped briskly into the dining-hall, rapped sharply on the galvanised side of the hut, and in the manner of an orderly officer, and with a broad smile, he said: "Any complaints?"

There was a roar of laughter from the men as they sprang up from their seats — laughter in which the King joined, sharing the enjoyment of his own joke.

There was a startling incident at Pentrebach, where a horse attached to a baker's van ran away while a number of children were using the vehicle as a grand-stand.

Attempts by local unemployed to stop the animal failed, and at length a Cardiff City constable, Police-constable James Taylor, checked the horse as it was dashing towards the dense crowd. The children were thrown off, one having to receive ambulance treatment.

Tragedy marked one stage of the tour. A well-known Trealaw woman collapsed as the King approached and died within a few minutes.

Amid cheering crowds at Dinas, Rhondda, after seeing the sports ground which has been made from an old colliery tip.

BOY WITH MIDDLE-AGED MIND

Brilliant Scholar's Suicide

Stated by his father to have the mind of a man of 40, Peter MacDonald Thomas, a 16-year-old schoolboy, whose headless body was discovered on the railway line, was found by the jury at a Barnsley inquest to-day to have committed suicide when mentally unbalanced.

The father, Ernest Thomas, a carpenter, said that although the boy was happy at school and played games he appeared to have advanced views.

The Coroner (Mr. C. J. Haworth) quoted from a letter written by the boy. "I had decided to die at least four weeks before this because I realise I was far too backward in everything, and I have no hope that I should be able to perform all that I desire i.e. in Greek, Latin, etc., in future."

The father said that in addition to his work at school the boy had done considerable studies on his own..

Mr. A. J. Schooling, headmaster of the school, said that the boy was perhaps the most brilliant boy in the school. He was very reserved and of placid temperament.

GERMAN PLANES MYSTERY

Eight Forced Down in Yugoslavia

Belgrade, Wednesday.—Within the last week eight German military aeroplanes have had forced landings in Yugoslavia.

They were military machines of recent types piloted by German officers in civil clothes and accompanied by military observers also in mufti. After taking their bearings and filling up with petrol all these machines left for Greece.

Official circles are silent and refuse to divulge the ultimate destination of the aeroplanes, but the popular suggestion is that they are bound for Spain.—Reuter.

ITALIAN REBUFF TO FRANCE

Germany's Denouncement of Treaty

Rome, Wednesday.—Italy has refused to join with France in a collective protest to Germany against the denunciation last Saturday of the navigational clauses of the Versailles Treaty.

M. Blondel, the French Charge d'Affaires, to-day asked Count Ciano, the Italian Foreign Minister, whether Italy would join in such a protest.

Count Ciano refused.—Reuter

REFUSED £400,000 FOR BUSINESS

—Died Worth £155

Reputed at one time to be a millionaire and to have refused £400,000 for his business, Sir James William Bulmer, who died in June intestate, has left £155.

He started work as an errand boy, later becoming a builder and finally one of the most notable personalities in the West Riding textile trade. He was the founder of Smith, Bulmer, and Co., Ltd., of Halifax.

Mr. MALCOLM STEWART

To Dine With the King To-night

Mr. Malcolm Stewart, whose outspoken report was the focal point of the all-night debate on the Special Areas in the House of Commons, has been commanded by the King to dine with him in South Wales to-night.

Mr. Stewart, who resigned from his position as Chief Commissioner for the Special Areas on presenting his report, will tell the King his plans for reviving the South Wales area when they meet. Thus the King, at the end of the first day of his tour in which he is seeing for himself the conditions in South Wales, will also have the advantage of Mr. Stewart's special knowledge of the area.

Mr. Stewart is travelling to Wales during the day.

LATEST NEWS

(SEE ALSO BACK PAGE)

Royal Visit

"Long Live Your Majesty To Help Us!"

(From Our Special Correspondent)

PENTREBACH, Wednesday.

The King began his tour promptly to time and drove straight to Boverton, where the Welsh Land Settlement Society have placed 70 unemployed miners and their families on a co-operative farm of 650 acres.

As he drove through an archway decorated with leeks the men and their families gathered in a square under the grey ruins of Boverton Castle cheered. Bare-headed and wearing a light grey overcoat, the King stepped quickly across the courtyard and was greeted by Mr. C. T. Bean, the manager.

As he passed down the line of waiting men he asked them details of their service on the land and singled out Mr. J. Dalton, who came to Boverton from Dowlais. Dalton was wearing a disabled ex-Service men's badge, and the King asked him what his injuries had been. Dalton told him.

What they said to one another is told in the first column of this page.

Thought for Invalids

The thought of the thousands of others of their countrymen who remain hopeless in the valleys of despair has been ever-present in the minds of those ordinary people whom the King has met to-day. Even the banners across the streets of the villages and towns have borne a message, typical of which was one I saw at Trethomas, "Live Long to Help Us." Another was, "We Appreciate Your Mission."

On the whole, the crowds which have lined the kerbs and hedgerows have been silent. There have been bursts of cheers, but one would believe that the King's errand is to bring people in these stricken valleys something from which hope may be born again and not a day's holiday for unrestrained rejoicing.

Perhaps for one little community, that at Crossways Hospital School, that thought does not apply. One of their number wrote to the King and asked him to slow down as he passed the school. The King promised that he would, and he kept his promise, for as the Royal procession passed the white-clad nurses and their tiny crippled charges lining the white roadway above Cowbridge the King's car slowed down. The King saluted the little patients, and their lungs well-nigh burst with the vigour of their acclamation.

A Shrug of the Shoulders

Here, at Pentrebach, the King has seen one of the Ministry of Labour's preparatory centres where unemployed men between the ages of 18 and 35 are prepared for training at a Government centre.

Old men who had laboured in the Dowlais Steelworks when the Bessemer turned out there what was reputed to be the finest in the world stood by the ruins of the blast furnaces to-day and sang Welsh hymns while they waited for the King to arrive.

When he did come they broke into the National Anthem, and the King halted for a moment. Then he hurriedly crossed a wooden bridge on to a clear site beneath a towering chimney stack. His first words were: "This is obsolete and derelict. I believe it is out of date."

"L.G.'s" MESSAGE

At Boverton the message which Mr. Lloyd George sent to the Commissioner of the Distressed Areas in South Wales was read to the King. The message read:

Please convey my loyal apologies to his Majesty for not being able to join as a Welsh M.P. and a member of your committee in welcoming him on his errand of mercy to the desolated areas of South Wales.

His visit is a message of hope which will add to the gratitude Welshmen have always felt for his continued interest in their well-being. I am glad he has been given the opportunity of seeing the admirable experiments in land settlement you are conducting at Boverton.

The following reply to their greetings has been received by the Cardiff Chamber of Trade:—

9.45, Llantwit Major (O.H.M.S.)—To the president of the Cardiff Chamber of Trade,—The King sincerely thanks the president and members of the Cardiff Chamber of Trade for their telegram of welcome to the special area which his Majesty much appreciates.—Ernest Brown, Ministry of Labour.

Mr. Charles Keen, who welcomed the Royal party, agreed.

The King turned, half to his left, and stared towards the cold furnaces. He said nothing for a long time—a very long time it seemed in the cold winter's afternoon.

Then he seemed to shrug his shoulders and turned away.

Staring up at the chimney stack, the King asked how it would be demolished. He was told, and then said: "It is a pity you could not do it to-day; then I might see how it is done."

He passed again the old men standing in the shadows of the blast furnaces and gave them a salute to themselves. Then he was gone.

ABERTILLERY FACILITIES

Mr. W. H. Gilson, proprietor of the Olwen Colliery, Abertillery, informed the *South Wales Echo* that members of the public may use the gardens near the colliery when the King visits the Glebe Sports Club, Abertillery, to-morrow. The gardens are near the sports club, which the King will inspect.

GREENOCK BY-ELECTION

Two Candidates Nominated

Two candidates were nominated to-day for the Greenock by-election caused by the death of Sir Godfrey Collins, Secretary for Scotland. They were:—

Mr. V. L. Cornelius (Lib.-Nat.);
Mr. R. Gibson, K.C. (Lab.).

Mr. Cornelius, whose home is in Surrey, is 34, and has had diplomatic experience. Mr. Gibson has previously fought North Edinburgh, Roxburgh, and Dundee.

At the last election the figures were:—

Sir G. Collins (Lib.-Nat.)	20,299
T. Irwin (Lab.)	16,945
J. L. Kinlock (Ind.)	1,286
Lib.-Nat. majority	3,354

Polling day has been fixed for Thursday, November 26.

MINISTER CALLED 'WAR DESERTER' KILLS HIMSELF

Man Whom French Chamber Vindicated

(From Reuter's Correspondent)

LILLE, Wednesday.

M. Salengro, Socialist Minister of the Interior, Mayor of Lille, and the man who was called a deserter in the French Chamber, committed suicide in dramatic circumstances to-day.

His body was found in his room. All the gas taps were on.

M. Salengro's brother declares that the Minister had been very much affected by several recent deaths in his family, including that of his wife, and by the recent attacks made upon him.

This, he says, led to his committing suicide.

M. Salengro was the original cause of the stormy debate in the Chamber at the end of last week which led to a free fight on the Floor of the House.

M. Salengro's War record had been called in question—allegations had been made that he was a deserter and not captured by the Germans.

The Findings

A special committee, composed of General Gamelin and expert representatives set up by M. Blum to inquire under conditions of a court-martial into the allegations that the Minister had been sentenced to death for desertion, found at the end of last month that the charge was baseless.

Its findings were:

(1) That M. Salengro was judged by only one War Council—not two, as alleged against him.

(2) That he was never sentenced to death.

(3) That he was acquitted by the War Council although a prisoner in Germany at the time and unable to defend himself.

Despite the result of the inquiry questions on M. Salengro's War record were put down in the Chamber, resulting on Friday last in one of the bitterest debates of recent French Parliamentary history.

Finally, a resolution was passed by 472 votes to 103 condemning the inanity of the accusations against a member of the Government and the defamatory charges

In addition to the strain imposed on him by these charges, M. Salengro, who was still in middle age and had great capacities for organisation, had not an easy time in managing the intern[al] situation since the coming to power [of] M. Blum's Government.

Great Responsibility

As Minister of the Interior he had to bear during the past five-and-a-half months the great responsibility of maintaining internal order; firstly, while the wave of "stay-in" strikes was sweeping over the country, and later when his task was complicated by reactions to the struggle in Spain.

He had been in poor health for some time, but when the great debate in which his honour was at stake took place last Friday he took his seat next to the Minister of Defence, a look of calm determination on his face.

M. Salengro, who was 46, was suffering from aortitis—denegeration of the main artery leading from the heart.

The Premier, M. Blum, went to Lille to-day to pay his last respects to his colleague and friend.

MRS. SIMPSON'S LIFE STORY: Page 5

WIRELESS: P. 20

DAILY SKETCH

MRS. SIMPSON PAGES OF PICTURES

No. 8,612　　　　FRIDAY, DECEMBER 4, 1936　　　　ONE PENNY

ROYAL FAMILY IN NIGHT CONFERENCE

The King Visits Queen Mary After Talks With Duke of York and Premier

'DAILY SKETCH' REPORTERS

THE King, after a day of crisis, after conferences with his Heir Presumptive, the Duke of York, with Mr. Baldwin, with secretaries and officials, drove to Marlborough House late last night and took part in a Royal family conference.

Queen Mary was there. So were the Duke and Duchess of York, the Duke and Duchess of Gloucester and the Duke of Kent.

It was almost 11 o'clock when the King's car arrived at Marlborough House. It was half an hour later when he left his mother and returned to the Palace. At 1.30 a.m. he left again for Fort Belvedere.

It was 12.15 a.m. before the Duke and Duchess of York left Marlborough House.

Earlier—at 8.30 p.m.—the King drove from the Fort to Buckingham Palace. In his private black saloon he drove in by one of the side entrances.

CROWDS MISS THE KING

Crowds who had waited patiently all day in the hope of catching a glimpse of him were disappointed.

But the crowds had seen the Duke of York arrive ten minutes earlier. He awaited the King, who went to him immediately he arrived.

They had a long talk together, then the Duke drove away alone.

The curious crowds began to dwindle. Some waited. Mr. Baldwin arrived, entered the Palace by the entrance usually reserved for Royalty, almost unnoticed.

He left the House of Commons in a police car shortly before nine o'clock, and arrived at the Palace at 9.15. He was immediately ushered into the King's presence, for his third interview in eight days.

ROYAL 'PLANE EXPECTED AT LE BOURGET

When Mr. Baldwin left the Palace his face was set and grave. He returned to Downing-street for a few minutes, then went to the House of Commons, where he went into conference with Mr. Malcolm MacDonald, Dominions Secretary; Mr. Te Water, High Commissioner for South Africa; and Mr. Vincent Massey, Canada's High Commissioner.

The Archbishop of Canterbury called at the House of Commons during the day. He remained with Mr. Baldwin for some time.

It is understood that the King's private aeroplane, piloted by Wing Commander Fielden, is awaited at Le Bourget Aerodrome to-day. Mrs. Simpson is expected on board.

Elaborate arrangements have already been made at Le Bourget to ensure absolute privacy on arrival of the 'plane. The hour of arrival is to be kept secret and no unauthorised person is to be allowed on the field.

CONTINUED ON BACK PAGE

This recent studio portrait of Mrs. Ernest Simpson shows her with one of her favourite pet dogs, a Cairn terrier.

MRS. SIMPSON PICTURES: 5, 16, 18, 19, 21, 23, 27, 32, 36

GOD SAVE THE KING

Daily Mirror

Registered at the G.P.O. as a newspaper.

No. 10302   Mon. Dec. 7, 1936   One Penny

45,000,000 DEMAND TO KNOW—

1. What, justly stated and in detail, is the King's request to his Cabinet?

2. What steps were taken to ascertain the views of the people of the Dominions and to explain to them the issues involved in this great crisis?

3. Is the British Cabinet prepared to approach the Governments of the Dominions with a frank request that they should reconsider their verdict against the King and consent to a marriage even if it involved new legislation?

4. Is the British Cabinet sure beyond doubt that the abdication of Edward VIII would not strike a terrible blow at the greatest institution in the world—our monarchy—and thereby cause irreparable harm?

5. Would the abdication of our King mean that he would be EXILED not only from Great Britain but also from every country in his Empire?

—and Then They Will Judge!

Daily Mirror

GOD SAVE THE KING!

TUESDAY
Dec. 8 No. 10302
ONE PENNY

MRS. SIMPSON READY TO GIVE UP THE KING

His Majesty Alone to Decide

Lord Brownlow, Lord-in-Waiting to the King, in a statement issued on behalf of Mrs. Simpson, at Cannes, last night, said:—

"Mrs. Simpson would desire, if such action could solve the problem, to withdraw immediately from a situation which has become both unhappy and untenable."

SEE PAGE THREE

THE AIR CLEARED

Mr. Baldwin Leaving Downing-street for the House to Make His Statement on the King

EARLIER IN THE DAY ANOTHER VITAL STATEMENT HAD BEEN MADE BY MR. BALDWIN IN THE HOUSE OF COMMONS. THIS PLACES THE NATION IN POSSESSION OF THE FACTS.

The question as to the King's request, which has been consistently pressed during the past few days, has been answered.

Now the air is clear—and the whole country knows the position.

His Majesty asked the Cabinet for their advice on the question of morganatic marriage—and on no other question. He wanted to know if it could be considered as a possible solution of the position in which he finds himself.

The Government have said that they are not prepared to introduce legislation to make such a marriage possible.

The Government have NOT said that they will not agree to marriage.

Already the Premier has stated that the King requires "no consent from any other authority to make his marriage legal."

The position, therefore, is this:—

The question of abdication need not arise.

The problem is clear—and now the decision rests with his Majesty.

It is neither necessary nor advisable for him to decide his course in haste. As Mr. Churchill has said, marriage can in no circumstances be accomplished for nearly five months.

And, it is understood too, that at no time has the suggestion been made that Mrs. Simpson should become Queen.

THE DAILY MIRROR, Wednesday, December 9, 1936.

Daily Mirror

No. 10304   Registered at the G.P.O as a newspaper.   ONE PENNY

The four men who were in a vital conference with the King last night

THE KING AND BROTHERS HAVE FIVE - HOUR CONFERENCE WITH MR. BALDWIN AT FORT

VITAL CONFERENCES BETWEEN THE KING, THE DUKE OF YORK, THE DUKE OF KENT, THE PREMIER, AND MR. WALTER MONCKTON, K.C., ATTORNEY-GENERAL TO THE DUCHY OF CORNWALL, LASTED FOR MORE THAN FIVE HOURS AT FORT BELVEDERE LAST NIGHT.

MR. BALDWIN ARRIVED AT FIVE O'CLOCK; DINED WITH THE KING, HIS BROTHERS, MR. MONCKTON AND SIR ERIC MIEVILLE, PRIVATE SECRETARY TO THE DUKE OF YORK, AND DID NOT LEAVE UNTIL 10.5. THE DUKE OF KENT HAD BEEN AT THE FORT THROUGHOUT THE DAY AND THE DUKE OF YORK ARRIVED AT 6.30; BOTH LEFT AT 11 O'CLOCK.

Police guards around the Fort were increased. Extra patrols on motor-cycles arrived, and the main road was cleared of all stationary traffic.

An important statement is expected to be made in the House of Commons this afternoon by Mr. Baldwin. Important information affecting the situation will, it is believed, be imparted to the Cabinet when they meet at Downing-street, this morning.

Downing Street Is Quiet

While the day's discussions were drawing to a close a specially chartered 'plane was landing in Marseilles after flying from London. The occupants of the 'plane, including a doctor and Mrs. Simpson's solicitor, left the aerodrome for Cannes by car.

Mr. Baldwin arrived at Downing-street from Fort Belvedere at eleven o'clock, accompanied by Captain Dugdale, Parliamentary Private Secretary.

There had been little activity in Downing-street during the day until shortly after four o'clock, when Mr. Baldwin left No. 10 with Sir Eric Mieville and Mr. Walter Monckton, K.C., for Fort Belvedere.

(Continued on back page)

M.P.s ARE GROWING MORE CHEERFUL

After M.P.s had for days grown resigned to the view that the abdication of the King was imminent, there was a sudden change in outlook last night. Many were convinced that a happier issue was in sight.

LAWYER IN AIR DASH TO CANNES

BY A SPECIAL CORRESPONDENT

After motoring ninety miles from Marseilles—where their air liner had landed—a London lawyer and a consultant arrived at Cannes at eleven o'clock last night. They will visit Mrs. Simpson to-day.

IN circumstances of strict secrecy an air liner ,on Government charter, left Croydon Aerodrome for Cannes yesterday morning.

Passengers were Dr. William Douglas Kirkwood, Mr. Theodore Goddard, a partner of Theodore Goddard and Co., solicitors, of Serjeants' Inn, London, who have acted for Mrs. Simpson, and Mr. Sidney Barron, solicitor's clerk.

Small attache cases were the passengers' only luggage.

The *Daily Mirror* understands that the aero plane was engaged with the co-operation of the Air Ministry.

Lord Brownlow stated at Cannes last night (says the British United Press): "Mr. Goddard is coming at Mrs. Simpson's suggestion to discuss details in regard to closing her London house. She has no intention of returning to London for a considerable time."

It is also believed that Mrs. Simpson will sign some important documents.

The liner took off from Croydon in spite of reports of bad weather over France.

Captain C. F. Almond, the pilot, landed first at Le Bourget, Paris, in the military part of the aerodrome, and a police guard prevented anyone from approaching.

Cordon of Gendarmes

Lyons was the next stop, and there, says Reuter, a cordon of gendarmes guarded the airport while officials awaited the liner's arrival.

Dr. W. D. Kirkwood is a well-known consultant, of Sloane-street, S.W.

On inquiry at his house yesterday the *Daily Mirror* was told that he was making no appointments, but that appointments could be made with Dr. Baldwin, his partner.

Since Mrs. Simpson arrived at Cannes there have been rumours that she is feeling the strain of recent events, and that her general health is unsatisfactory.

MRS. SIMPSON

A striking photograph of Mrs. Simpson, for which she posed yesterday, is on page 15.

43

Evening Standard

To-morrow's Weather—
Rather cold. SEE PAGE THREE.

Lighting-up Time
To-night 4.19.

No. 35,036   LONDON, THURSDAY, DECEMBER 10, 1936   ONE PENNY

THE KING ABDICATES
Duke of York Monarch

THE following message from his Majesty King Edward VIII. was read in the House of Commons this afternoon by the Speaker:

AFTER LONG AND ANXIOUS CONSIDERATION I HAVE DETERMINED TO RENOUNCE THE THRONE TO WHICH I SUCCEEDED ON THE DEATH OF MY FATHER, AND I AM COMMUNICATING THIS, MY FINAL AND IRREVOCABLE DECISION.

REALISING AS I DO THE GRAVITY OF THIS STEP, I CAN ONLY HOPE THAT I SHALL HAVE THE UNDERSTANDING OF MY PEOPLES IN THE DECISION I HAVE TAKEN AND THE REASONS WHICH HAVE LED ME TO TAKE IT.

I WILL NOT ENTER NOW INTO MY PRIVATE FEELINGS, BUT I WOULD BEG THAT IT SHOULD BE REMEMBERED THAT THE BURDEN WHICH CONSTANTLY RESTS UPON THE SHOULDERS OF A SOVEREIGN IS SO HEAVY THAT IT CAN ONLY BE BORNE IN CIRCUMSTANCES DIFFERENT FROM THOSE IN WHICH I NOW FIND MYSELF.

I CONCEIVE THAT I AM NOT OVERLOOKING THE DUTY THAT RESTS ON ME TO PLACE IN THE FOREFRONT THE PUBLIC INTERESTS WHEN I DECLARE THAT I AM CONSCIOUS THAT I CAN NO LONGER DISCHARGE THIS HEAVY TASK WITH EFFICIENCY OR WITH SATISFACTION TO MYSELF.

I HAVE ACCORDINGLY THIS MORNING EXECUTED AN INSTRUMENT OF ABDICATION IN THE TERMS FOLLOWING :—

I, EDWARD VIII. OF GREAT BRITAIN, IRELAND, AND THE BRITISH DOMINIONS BEYOND THE SEAS, KING, EMPEROR OF INDIA, DO HEREBY DECLARE MY IRREVOCABLE DETERMINATION TO RENOUNCE THE THRONE FOR MYSELF AND FOR MY DESCENDANTS, AND MY DESIRE THAT EFFECT SHOULD BE GIVEN TO THIS INSTRUMENT OF ABDICATION IMMEDIATELY.

IN TOKEN WHEREOF I HAVE HEREUNTO SET MY HAND THIS TENTH DAY OF DECEMBER, NINETEEN HUNDRED AND THIRTY-SIX IN THE PRESENCE OF THE WITNESSES WHOSE SIGNATURES ARE SUBSCRIBED.

EDWARD R.I.

MY EXECUTION OF THIS INSTRUMENT HAS BEEN WITNESSED BY MY THREE BROTHERS, THEIR ROYAL HIGHNESSES THE DUKE OF YORK, THE DUKE OF GLOUCESTER, AND THE DUKE OF KENT.

I DEEPLY APPRECIATE THE SPIRIT WHICH HAS ACTUATED THE APPEALS WHICH HAVE BEEN MADE TO ME TO TAKE A DIFFERENT DECISION, AND I HAVE, BEFORE REACHING MY FINAL DETERMINATION, MOST FULLY PONDERED OVER THEM.

BUT MY MIND IS MADE UP.

MOREOVER, FURTHER DELAY CANNOT BUT BE MOST INJURIOUS TO THE PEOPLES WHOM I HAVE TRIED TO SERVE AS PRINCE OF WALES AND AS KING, AND WHOSE FUTURE HAPPINESS AND PROSPERITY ARE THE CONSTANT WISH OF MY HEART.

I TAKE LEAVE OF THEM IN THE CONFIDENT HOPE THAT THE COURSE WHICH I HAVE THOUGHT IT RIGHT TO FOLLOW IS THAT WHICH IS BEST FOR THE STABILITY OF THE THRONE AND EMPIRE AND THE HAPPINESS OF MY PEOPLES.

I AM DEEPLY SENSIBLE OF THE CONSIDERATION WHICH THEY HAVE ALWAYS EXTENDED TO ME BOTH BEFORE AND AFTER MY ACCESSION TO THE THRONE, AND WHICH I KNOW THEY WILL EXTEND IN FULL MEASURE TO MY SUCCESSOR.

I AM MOST ANXIOUS THAT THERE SHOULD BE NO DELAY OF ANY KIND IN GIVING EFFECT TO THE INSTRUMENT WHICH I HAVE EXECUTED, AND THAT ALL NECESSARY STEPS SHOULD BE TAKEN IMMEDIATELY TO SECURE THAT MY LAWFUL SUCCESSOR, MY BROTHER, HIS ROYAL HIGHNESS THE DUKE OF YORK, SHOULD ASCEND THE THRONE.

EDWARD R.I.

The Prime Minister told the House how King Edward came to his decision—

See Page Two

FRIDAY, JUNE 4, 1937

Daily Mirror

No. 10453   Registered at the G.P.O. as a Newspaper.   ONE PENNY

...The Duke and Duchess of Windsor...
ON THE STEPS OF A
NEW LIFE—TOGETHER

His Royal Highness the Duke of Windsor and his bride, Mrs. Wallis Warfield, walking down to the terrace of the Chateau de Cande at Tours—their first public appearance after their wedding yesterday.

Daily Mirror

BRITAIN'S BIGGEST DAILY SALE

3p   Monday, May 29, 1972   ✦ ✦ ✦   No. 21,268

Royal love story ends with the Duchess at his side

Born to be King

HIS LAST WISH

'Bury me at Windsor'

By NICK DAVIES

THE Duke of Windsor, who died in Paris early yesterday with his beloved Duchess by his side, has had his last wish granted by the Queen — the wish to be buried at Windsor.

The Duchess, for whose love he gave up the British Throne, will stay at Buckingham Palace—at the special invitation of the Queen—during the funeral period.

This will be the first time that the 75-year-old Duchess has been invited to stay at the Palace.

She will be driven there after escorting her husband's body to Windsor Castle on Wednesday.

She is expected to stay at least until the following Tuesday—the day after the funeral.

A RAF VC-10 will fly the Duke's body from Paris to RAF Benson, Oxfordshire, on Wednesday morning.

The Duchess will travel in the plane, which will be met by the Duke and Duchess of Kent.

State

The body will then be taken to Windsor Castle, where it will lie in state in St. George's Chapel on Friday and Saturday.

This will be open to the public. It is also likely to be seen on television.

The funeral service will be private and will be held in the chapel on Monday morning.

About 200 people only will be allowed into the chapel for the service, but reporters and cameramen will be allowed.

The interment will take place in the afternoon at the tiny burial ground at Frogmore in Windsor's Little Park. This will be attended only by the immediate family.

Frogmore is where Queen Victoria, Prince Albert and the Duke's brother, the Duke of Kent, killed during the second world war, are buried.

The three British monarchs since Queen Victoria have all been buried in St. George's Chapel. They are interred in the vaults.

But the Duke of Windsor did not wish to be buried there.

Many years ago, he made arrange-

QUEEN ASKS WIDOW: STAY AT PALACE

ments with his brother, who succeeded him to the throne as King George VI, that he should be buried at Frogmore. And this request was also agreed to recently by the Queen.

The fact that the Duke will be lying in state at St. George's Chapel and not at Westminster Hall in London gave rise to protests last night.

Since Edward VII died in 1910, it has become a tradition that every British monarch lies in state in Westminster Hall, symbolising the close links between the monarchy and Parliament.

Lord Greenwood, the former chairman of the Labour Party, said last night:

"I remember seeing the Duke of Windsor with his three brothers—the Dukes of York, Gloucester and Kent—standing guard in Westminster Hall at the lying in state of their father, King George V.

"I am sure that many people would like the opportunity of paying tribute

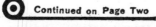
Continued on Page Two

Happy together . . . the Duke and Duchess at their Paris home in March, 1969.

WHAT THE MIRROR SAYS—Page 2: PRINCE . . KING . . EXILE—Pages 13, 14 & 15

Daily Mirror

BRITAIN'S BIGGEST DAILY SALE

3p   Tuesday, June 6, 1972   +   No. 21,275

EXIT THE WOMAN WHO MADE HISTORY

THE Duchess of Windsor says goodbye to Britain . . . barely an hour after the burial of her husband.

Slowly she climbs the steps to her aircraft at London's Heathrow Airport, heading for Paris and for home. Alone now in her grief. The Duchess, whose love for a king changed the course of history, had slipped away without fuss after the interment in Windsor Great Park.

There were brief farewells to the Royal Family, privately, in Windsor Castle. But no time even for a cup of tea. No member of the Royal Family went to Heathrow to see her off. But as a Buckingham Palace spokesman explained: "This was not in any way a slight. The Queen never goes to the airport for anybody."

It is a sorrowful parting just the same. An exit tinged with grief . . . with the same eternal shadow of sadness that made her romance one of the great love stories of history.

Picture by VICTOR CRAWSHAW

Three-page special: Pages 13, 14 and 15

CHAPTER 4

GEORGE VI

The Press portrayed the King as a rallying point for his people.

Edward's younger brother, the Duke of York, had no wish to become King. A shy man, afflicted by a pronounced stammer, he protested to his friend Louis Mountbatten that he had no training for the job. His wife, the former Lady Elizabeth Bowes-Lyon, was even more aghast at the enormity of what had happened.

But "Bertie" showed decisiveness even in his first few difficult days. His first act was to dispense with his own Christian name, Albert, in favour of his father's — with an eye to stability and continuity. He also chose the name by which his brother would be known in his self-imposed exile, and adamantly refused to accord his wife the style and dignity of Royal Highness — something which the Windsors never forgave. The news quite spoilt their wedding day in France the following summer. "What a damnable wedding present," the Duke said to his guests.

The new King George VI also overruled suggestions that he should delay the customary year or so before being crowned in Westminster Abbey. The arrangements for his brother's coronation were already well in hand, and he saw no need to undo them. "Same day," he told the Lord Chamberlain, "different King."

On the balcony that May day, just six months after the abdication trauma, the *Daily Sketch* front page (p.53) gives pride of place to old Queen Mary, as proud of this son as she was ashamed of the other. Suddenly, too, those little princesses whose childhood had so entranced the nation were wearing little crowns. Elizabeth had become heir presumptive.

A glimpse of the happy family life which had been so rudely interrupted is seen in the wistful Marcus Adams portrait which led the *Sunday Graphic's* Coronation issue (p.54). There was another dramatic assassination attempt, and Queen Mary was involved in a car crash, but most of the Royal news was better than the year before.

Having already scored a great hit on a State visit to France (p.55), the King and Queen went down even better in the United States, where their visit to the Roosevelt White House prompted the *News Chronicle* (p.56) to award them a "success unique in the annals of modern constitutional monarchy".

On the horizon, however, was the grim prospect of war in Europe. At its beginning, as throughout its progress, the press portrayed the King as a rallying point for his people. It is interesting to see how his message to the nation dominated the *Daily Sketch's* historic announcement, in September 1939,

that war had been declared (p.57).

Memories of the Royal visit to America had the New York *Journal-American* leading on September 13, 1940 with the news that the King and Queen had survived the bombing of Buckingham Palace (p.58).

The King's youngest brother, the Duke of Kent, was not so lucky. In August 1942 news arrived of his death in a flying accident while on active duty (p.59). It was just three weeks since the christening of his and Princess Marina's third child, Prince Michael.

In 1945 the King was again the keynote of the Press's victory coverage. Victory in Europe merited an appearance by all the family on the balcony of Buckingham Palace, which the *Daily Sketch* chose to promote above a pictures of the victorious allied commanders. A year later, Queen Mary was again prominent on the Royal podium at the Victory Parade.

One more year, and Britain's post-war blues were dispelled by news of a Royal engagement. Still couponed, still rationed, still devastated by the Blitz, the nation needed some good news — and the King and Queen managed to lay it on with the announcement that their "dearly beloved daughter" Elizabeth was to marry a Prince described by the papers as a "dashing blond Viking" — Philip of Greece and Denmark, alias Lieutenant Philip Mountbatten RN.

The wedding that November afforded a brief national knees-up amid the continuing recovery from war. As life for the average citizen remained pretty grim, the Royal Family kept laying on causes for celebration: the King and Queen's silver wedding anniversary in April 1948 — and the birth, that November, of a Prince in direct line of succession. "A girdle of rejoicing," declared the *Daily Graphic* had been "thrown round the world" by the arrival on the scene of Prince Charles.

Christening portraits, first birthday portraits and news, two years later, that young Charles now had a sister kept the papers as busy with Royal stories as they were in the early 1980s. The happy young family growing around Elizabeth and Philip signalled a new mood in monarchy — more relaxed, less stuffy, more down-to-earth than of old. The institution had come a long way since Edward VIII's abdication brought it to its knees only 15 years before.

But the transport of Royal delight was abruptly halted early in 1952. As rainswept commuters poured out of a London tube station, they divided into two respectful streams to avoid treading on a fallen newspaper placard proclaiming: THE KING IS DEAD.

THE DAILY MIRROR, Thursday, April 26, 1923.

FIRST ROYAL WEDDING NUMBER: PAGES OF SPECIAL PICTURES AND NEW SERIAL

The Daily Mirror

24 PAGES

NET SALE MUCH THE LARGEST OF ANY DAILY PICTURE NEWSPAPER

No. 6,076. — Registered at the G.P.O. as a Newspaper. — THURSDAY, APRIL 26, 1923 — One Penny.

TO-DAY'S GREAT ABBEY WEDDING

To-day London's gala week reaches its climax in the wedding of the Duke of York, second son of the King and Queen, to Lady Elizabeth Bowes-Lyon, youngest daughter of the Earl and Countess of Strathmore and Kinghorne, in the stately setting of Westminster Abbey. Favourable weather is alone required to ensure the unqualified success of the occasion as a national festival. Of the good wishes of all classes the Duke and his bride are heartily assured.

LADY DUFF GORDON WRITES EXCLUSIVELY ON FASHION in P. 10

DAILY SKETCH

INCORPORATING THE DAILY GRAPHIC

No. 6,095. | [Registered as a Newspaper.] | WEDNESDAY, OCTOBER 24, 1928 | ONE PENNY.

TWO MORE £250 CLAIMS PAID

PRINCESS ELIZABETH: NEW PHOTOGRAPHS

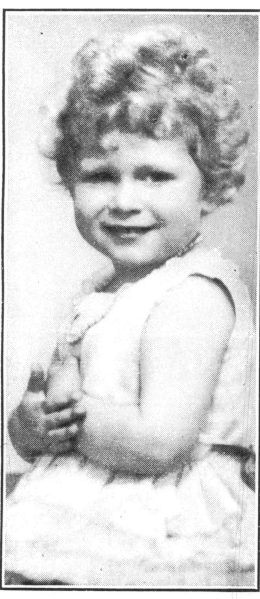

A smile that goes well with her light blue eyes and flaxen hair.

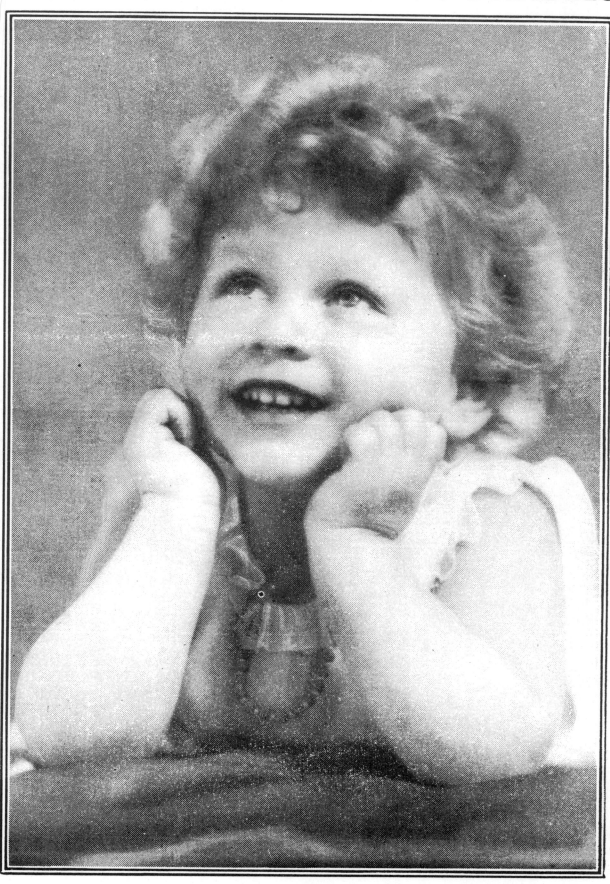

These new photographs of the Duchess of York and Princess Elizabeth show how the winning manner of the mother lives again in the child. The Princess, who will be three years old next April, says her name is " Lillybet."—(Marcus Adams.)

MANY MORE INSURANCE CLAIMS PAID TO-DAY

WIRELESS PROGRAMMES ON PAGE 17

Daily Mirror

THE DAILY PICTURE PAPER WITH THE LARGEST NET SALE

No. 8,406   Registered at the G.P.O. as a Newspaper.   TUESDAY, OCTOBER 28, 1930   One Penny

£100 CROSSWORD PUZZLE

PRINCESS MARGARET—FIRST PICTURE

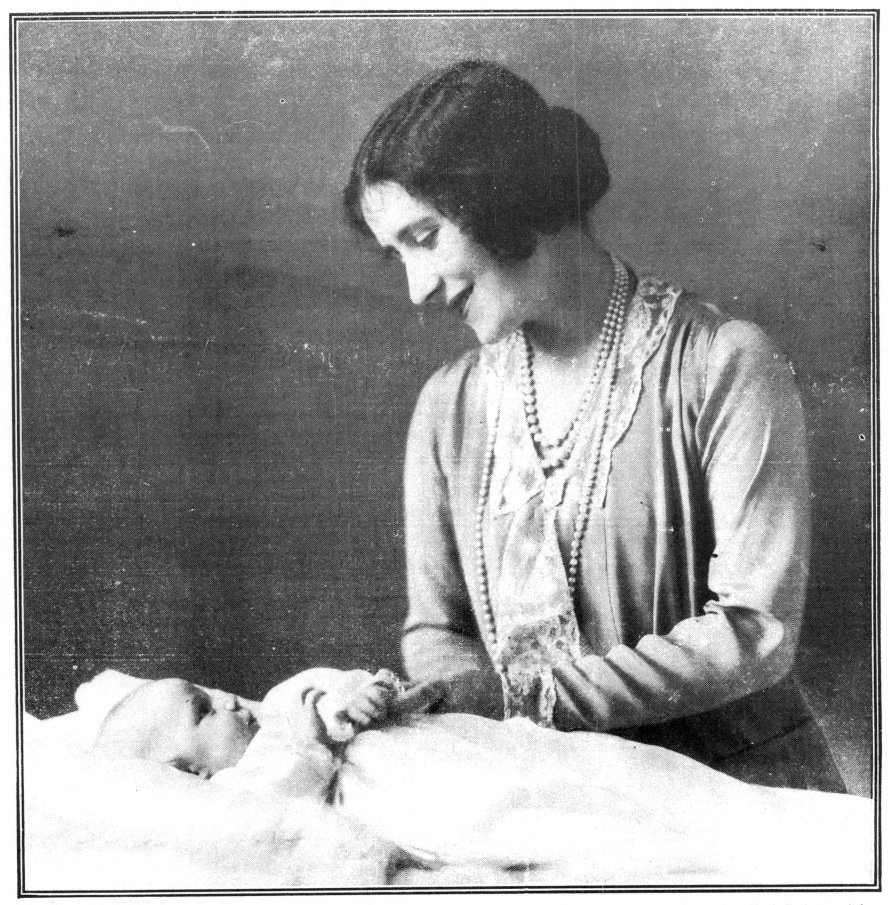

The Duchess of York with her second daughter, Princess Margaret Rose of York, the fourth grandchild of the King and Queen. A happy and contented baby, Princess Margaret has endeared herself to all visitors to her parents' Piccadilly home, whither she was brought with her little sister, Princess Elizabeth, from Glamis Castle to await her christening on Thursday in the private chapel of Buckingham Palace. This and other pictures on pages 12 and 13 are the first photographs of the baby Princess.

Daily Express

TODAY'S WEATHER : UNSETTLED, COLD.

RADIO PROGRAMMES : PAGE 23.

NO. 11,412 FRIDAY, DECEMBER 11, 1936 ONE PENNY

The King Abdicates: Duke Of York On The Throne
Baldwin Tells Commons The Whole Sad Story

GEORGE THE SIXTH

To be crowned on May 12—in place of his brother

Edward

The eighth King Edward of England, who is forty-two, renounces the Throne and becomes plain Mr. Windsor. His abdication was announced yesterday in a Message to Parliament in which he said:—

"After long and anxious consideration I have determined to renounce the Throne . . . and I am now communicating this my final and irrevocable decision."

The Message is given in full on Page Two. The Abdication Bill, which gives effect to King Edward's decision, is on Page Six.

THE NEW KING RETURNING TO HIS PICCADILLY HOME FROM FORT BELVEDERE JUST BEFORE MIDNIGHT.
See also Back Page.

Albert

The Duke of York, who is forty-one on Monday and is the second son of King George and Queen Mary, will be proclaimed King tomorrow. He will most probably take the title King George VI.

His accession makes the Duchess of York Queen and ten-year-old Princess Elizabeth the Heir to the Throne.

The new Queen will be England's first Queen Elizabeth since 1603.

'MR. WINDSOR' TO BROADCAST AT 10 TONIGHT

SITTING AT HIS STUDY DESK IN HIS COUNTRY HOME, FORT BELVEDERE, WITH HIS THREE BROTHERS—THE DUKE OF YORK, THE DUKE OF GLOUCESTER AND THE DUKE OF KENT—BY HIS SIDE, KING EDWARD AT TEN O'CLOCK YESTERDAY MORNING SIGNED THE "INSTRUMENT OF ABDICATION" WHICH LATER WAS READ IN EVERY PARLIAMENT OF THE BRITISH EMPIRE.

At that moment in the silent house where, in the words of the message which accompanied the announcement of his decision, he had spent so many days of "long and anxious consideration," the flag of the Duchy of Cornwall flying from the battlements was lowered from the masthead. With a stroke of the pen Edward Albert Christian George Andrew Patrick David had resigned his many titles and dignities to his brother, Albert Frederick Arthur George, Duke of York, and become plain "Mr. Windsor."

The shortest reign—325 days—in 453 years of England's history had been ended by the first of her Kings to give up his throne voluntarily. The Act of Abdication as passed by both Houses of Parliament today will be taken to Fort Belvedere for King Edward to sign this evening.

EXILE IN ITALY

That will be his last work as Monarch. Then, at about 10 p.m., he will, as "Mr. Windsor," broadcast a personal farewell to his peoples in Britain and the Dominions with an expression of his allegiance to the new Sovereign : after that he will leave the country, probably tomorrow morning. There is little doubt that a dukedom will be conferred on him, "Duke of Windsor" was the suggested title.

The probability is that he will live, for a time, in Italy ; it is reported that inquiries on his behalf are being made for a villa in Amalfi. He is not likely to return to England until after the Coronation, which it is thought will take place, as arranged, on May 12 next year.

The title to be assumed by the new

☞ PAGE TWO, COLUMN ONE

INDEX

New King Is Held Up By Cheering Crowds

MIDNIGHT VISIT TO MOTHER

WHEN the new King returned from Fort Belvedere to his home in Piccadilly at 11.40 last night he was greeted by a great multitude, which completely blocked the road. As his car drove into the forecourt cheer after cheer was raised, and there were shouts of "We want the King."

Men in evening dress crowded round. Women pressed their faces to the windows of the car, and were rewarded with a friendly smile.

After the new King had stepped out he turned to the crowd and raised his hat several times.

After he had gone into his house a man in the crowd started to sing the National Anthem. Immediately hundreds of people took it up.

The new King was clearly exhausted by the stress and anxieties of the last few hours, and it was to his wife that he hurried at once to explain fully all that had happened.

While their parents talked the little Princesses were asleep in their room overhead. Earlier in the day Princess Elizabeth had been told something of the situation. She went to bed with the knowledge that she is Heir Presumptive to the Throne.

At ten minutes after midnight the new King went to see his mother at Marlborough House. It was not until 1.35 that he left.

King 'Phones Mrs. Simpson

Daily Express Staff Reporter

CANNES, Thursday Night.

MRS. SIMPSON heard of the King's "final and irrevocable" decision to abdicate several hours before the world heard. The King himself told her.

The telephone rang in the Villa Lou Viei, Cannes, where Mrs. Simpson is staying. Lord Brownlow, Lord-in-Waiting to the King, answered it.

"The King, madam," he said.

Mrs. Simpson went to the 'phone. As she answered quietly, in monosyllables, her eyes filled with tears. The conversation went on for twenty minutes. Tears rolled down her face.

"Yes" and "No" were all Lord Brownlow and Mr. and Mrs. Herman Rogers (Mrs. Simpson's host and hostess) heard. She hung up the receiver, gave no explanation, said nothing, but for some time sat quietly waiting in an armchair.

Every one in the villa knew that the King had spoken to her.

All the day she had been silent and tearful, eating nothing, smoking rapidly, unable to read.

Later she spoke to the King again from the lounge of the villa. Every one left the room. When they returned they found her a little more composed.

The news of the abdication came dramatically to the villa. With some vague expectancy, a dozen Press men and women drifted down

☞ PAGE TWO, COLUMN THREE

LATEST NEWS
Telephone : Central 8000

REPORT THAT KING MAY LIVE IN ARGENTINE

Buenos Aires, Thursday.—Report is current here that King Edward has already negotiated for acquisition of an estate near Venado Tureto, Central Argentina. This district is known as "The Home of Argentine Polo" and possesses many luxury estancias.

If he should decide to live here, the King would be assured of wonderful welcome.—Reuter.

DAILY SKETCH

No. 8,746   THURSDAY, MAY 13, 1937   ONE PENNY

HISTORY IN PICTURES

The King and Queen on the Palace Balcony with Queen Mary and Princess Elizabeth smilingly acknowledging the people's cheers

WONDERFUL MATANIA ABBEY PICTURE

SUNDAY GRAPHIC
and SUNDAY NEWS

No. 1,153.   SUNDAY, MAY 9, 1937.   TWOPENCE.

SOUVENIR NUMBER

QUEEN—WIFE—MOTHER
The Finest Portrait of Her Majesty Ever Taken

The "Sunday Graphic" publishes to-day the finest picture ever taken of the Queen with Princess Elizabeth and Princess Margaret Rose. Every mother will treasure it as a wonderful expression of the love and devotion which surrounds the King in his family life.

—*(Marcus Adams.)*

DAILY SKETCH

No. 9,114   WEDNESDAY, JULY 20, 1938   ONE PENNY

Plainly pleased by the great welcome to them—the King and Queen, with President Lebrun, in Paris. The State visit finds its souvenir in pages of memorable pictures, telling the whole story, in to-day's " Daily Sketch."

News ✠ Chronicle

SOUVENIR OF THE ROYAL TOUR

FULL RECORD IN WORDS AND PICTURES

It Was A Brilliant Success

BEYOND any doubt the royal tour of Canada and America was a brilliant personal and diplomatic success, unique in the annals of modern constitutional Monarchy.

The overwhelming and instantaneous response of the Canadian people took statesmen and political observers on this side completely by surprise. Almost the entire population of Canada must have seen the King and Queen in the last month.

Hundreds of thousands of children, who had been saving their money cent by cent for many weeks, were taken in trains or in road trucks hundreds of miles for one brief glimpse of King George and Queen Elizabeth. Public enthusiasm was as great in the remote villages as in the large towns, and never flagged from the first moment to the last.

I have not seen anything in England to match this nation-wide demonstration of loyal fervour. The personal bearing of the King and Queen played a large part in a triumphant achievement. They made it clear that they were thoroughly enjoying the experience. They behaved perfectly because they behaved naturally.

The physical presence of the King of England transformed him at once into the King of Canada. The influence of this visit will be felt in the Dominion for years to come.

The success of the visit to the United States, though different, was scarcely less striking. It obliterated the bad impression caused by a clumsy ambassadorial handling of preliminaries ; and wrung praise from the most suspicious and cynical political quarters in the States.

The King and Queen played up splendidly and gave an admirable lesson in modest, democratic dignity to the fussy English officials, and, perhaps, to not a few royalty-ridden Americans.

There was not one untoward incident throughout the visit. The cheering—such cheering as had never been heard in any part of the States—seemed to signify in a special sense American democracy's warm understanding of British democracy's formidable task in Europe.

By A. J. Cummings, who represented the News Chronicle on the Royal Tour.

AND NOW MAY GOD DEFEND THE RIGHT: See P. 11

DAILY SKETCH

No. 9,464   MONDAY, SEPTEMBER 4, 1939   ONE PENNY

LATEST WAR NEWS

The King's Message

"STAND calm, firm and united!" That was the keynote of the message broadcast by the King to the Empire last night.

"In this grave hour," said the King, "perhaps the most fateful in our history, I send to every household of my people, both at home and overseas, this message, spoken with the same depth of feeling for each one of you as if I were able to cross your threshold and speak to you myself.

"For the second time in the lives of most of us we are at war.

"Over and over again we have tried to find a peaceful way out of the differences between ourselves and those who are now our enemies.

"But it has been in vain. We have been forced into a conflict. For we are called, with our Allies, to meet the challenge of a principle which, if it were to prevail, would be fatal to any civilised order in the world.

"It is the principle which permits a state, in the selfish pursuit of power, to disregard its treaties and its solemn pledges; which sanctions the use of force, or threat of force, against the sovereignty and independence of other states.

Must Meet The Challenge

"Such a principle, stripped of all disguise, is surely the mere primitive doctrine that might is right; and if this principle were established throughout the world, the freedom of our own country and of the whole British Commonwealth of Nations would be in danger.

"But far more than this—the peoples of the world would be kept in the bondage of fear, and all hopes of settled peace and of the security of justice and liberty among nations would be ended.

"This is the ultimate issue which confronts us. For the sake of all that we ourselves hold dear, and of the world's order and peace, it is unthinkable that we should refuse to meet the challenge.

"It is to this high purpose that I now call my people at home and my peoples across the seas, who will make our cause their own. I ask them to stand calm, firm and united in this time of trial.

"The task will be hard. There may be dark days ahead, and war can no longer be confined to the battlefield. But we can only do the right as we see the right, and reverently commit our cause to God.

"If one and all we keep resolutely faithful to it, ready for whatever service or sacrifice it may demand, then, with God's help, we shall prevail.

"May He bless and keep us all."

A copy of the message, with a facsimile of the King's signature will be sent to every home in the land.

The King about to broadcast last night.

Britain (since 11 a.m. yesterday) and France (since 5 p.m.) at war with Germany

Lord Gort leads British Expeditionary Force

Churchill in War Cabinet as First Lord

Hitler goes to the Front

Poles invade East Prussia

Warsaw alleges Germans are dropping gas bombs

LATE MESSAGES ON BACK PAGE

Blast Toll at 35; Probes On

LARGEST EVENING CIRCULATION IN AMERICA

CHARACTER QUALITY · New York · ENTERPRISE ACCURACY

Journal AND American

AN AMERICAN PAPER FOR THE AMERICAN PEOPLE

No. 19,262—DAILY

In Two Sections—Section One

FRIDAY, SEPTEMBER 13, 1940

Copyright, 1940, by King Features Syndicate, Inc. | DAILY 3 Cents | SATURDAY 5 Cents | SUNDAY 10 Cents

B

5

7TH SPORT WALL ST. CLOSING

KING, QUEEN SAFE IN PALACE BOMBING

Scalise Case Goes to Jury

A blue ribbon General Sessions Jury retired to deliberate the fate of former union leader George Scalise at 11:27 a. m. today after the grand larceny charges against him had been drastically reduced in a surprise ruling by Judge Schurman.

In charging the jurymen, who have been sitting in the Supreme Court Building for five weeks, Judge Schurman submitted only 10 of the original 60 counts of the trial indictment.

COULD GET 160 YEARS.

The ex-president of the Building Service Employes' International Union, who once served a prison term for white slavery, could still be sentenced to 160 years if convicted on the remaining counts.

These consisted of six counts of grand larceny, accusing Scalise of swindling his union of $12,519.27, and four counts of forgery in the third degree.

Thirty-five of the original 60 counts had been eliminated on motion of Assistant District Attorney Murray I. Gurfein. Judge Schurman ruled out another 15 counts.

The indictment originally charged the one-time Brooklyn undertaker who became head of the international union without an election of stealing $60,087 paid into the organization's treasury as

Continued on Page 9, Column 2.

Blast Origin Baffles Inquiry

(Pictures on Pages 16 and 17.)

A resolution for a Congressional investigation of possible sabotage at the blast-wrecked Hercules Powder Co. plant in Kenvil, N. J., was introduced in the House of Representatives at Washington today as the death toll reached 35 and may yet approach 50.

Rep. Anderson, Missouri Democrat, demanded that a committee of five be named by the House to conduct hearings and determine "if there is evidence of sabotage in this or in other national defense plants."

"RELATIVELY SAFE."

The mystery surrounding the blast's origin was intensified when G. W. Hunt, plant director, declared 10 tons of smokeless powder was destroyed in the catastrophe, adding:

"Smokeless powder is supposed to be relatively safe. I can't account for the explosion. We have found no evidence of sabotage, but that doesn't mean we won't investigate the possibility thoroughly. The damage exceeds $1,000,000."

COUNTS 35 BODIES.

The latest estimate of loss of life in the devastating explosion was made shortly before noon by Dr. H. Raymond Mutchler, Morris

Continued on Page 16, Column 1.

This photo-diagram of Buckingham Palace shows how the great building, home of Kings and Queens of England, was under attack today from the Nazi air raiders for the second time in three days. Their Majesties' private chapel (A) small building surrounded by pillars, was completely wrecked by one great bomb. Two more fell (B) in the quadrangle, tearing great craters in the paving and damaging the surrounding walls. Front of the palace, at top of picture, was pitted by another pair of bombs (C) that fell between the statue of Queen Victoria and the front entrance, facing east toward St. James' Park. Dotted lines show portion of palace damaged Tuesday. Building shown at bottom of picture with area inside dotted lines is the conservatory, swimming pool demolished in first assault on the palace.

Kelly Tells How He'll Toughen U.S.

By GEROLD FRANK, N. Y. Journal and American Staff Correspondent.

PHILADELPHIA, Sept. 13.—John B. Kelly, former Olympic champion, given the job of "toughening up" America by President Roosevelt, today outlined a drastic mass physical education program for national defense which will affect virtually every able-bodied man and woman from 18 to 70.

Nationwide in scope, the program will see the country divided into "physical health" districts, thousands of men and women joining in mass calisthenics, free medical clinics for physical examinations, hiking clubs patterned after those in Europe, and athletic meets in which all members of the family will participate.

"We've been living a life of ease," Kelly declared. "We've gone soft in this country. It won't be any easy job to harden us up.

"But we'll combine the best features of the physical training programs in Europe during the last 10 years. We'll copy them to our own advantage and get down to earth.

"I'm going to work under the slogan:

"'It's unpatriotic to be unhealthy!'"

Pointing to the great Czech Sokol organizations, Kelly said he hoped to have thousands of persons meet regularly at various stadiums throughout the county for exercises and calesthenics.

So that there will be no ques-

Continued on Page 9, Column 1.

Japs Mass Ships Off Indo-China

HONGKONG, Sept. 13 (By International News Service).—Japanese warships were reported massing in the Gulf of Tonkin today for what was believed to be an attack on French Indo-China.

Besides the warships, which were reported to number 120 vessels, 200 other warships and transports were said to be gathered at Waichow and at Hainan Island, just off the Indo-China coast.

Role of U. S. Planes In British Battles!

Airplanes are Great Britain's first line of defense against Hitler's blitzkrieg, and Britain has been buying planes from American manufacturers, as international law permits.

For "inside comment" on this aspect of the war, read Paul Mallon's column, "The News Behind the News," today on the page opposite the Editorial Page.

3 More Attacks Hammer London

LONDON, Sept. 13.—London fought off three waves of Nazi raiders today following another all-night assault which was beaten off by the capital's newly-perfected anti-aircraft system.

The first of the three alarms sounded at 7:45 a. m. (2:45 a. m. New York) and lasted 57 minutes. During the second alarm, which came at 9:45 a. m. and lasted four hours and ten minutes, Nazi raiders succeeded in scoring hits on Buckingham Palace and dropping incendiaries in Downing st. The third alarm, which lasted 18 minutes, was sounded at 3:52 p. m.

Fears of heavy casualties when a bomb struck a school during the second raid were dispelled when investigation showed the building was almost empty.

Long duration of the second raid compelled Home Defense authorities hastily to reorganize shelter plans in the crowded business and shopping districts. Even subways were pressed into use.

Anti-aircraft batteries fought a three-hour intermittent battle with planes on both sides of the Thames Estuary. Most of the planes were compelled to stay on the other side of the guns' "curtain of steel," but occasionally a hit-and-run raider

shot through the defenses to make a darting attack on London.

A shower of incendiary bombs fell on the central London area. An undetermined number of children were in the school when the building was struck, informed quarters said.

At the same time it was learned

Continued on Page 2, Column 1.

Flicker Fun

Selecting your flicker fun is made easy by the Journal-American amusement pages. No need to phone if you want to know what movies are featured at your neighborhood theatres. Just consult the Skouras Movie Guide and the announcements of other leading theatres that appear daily in this newspaper.

Raider Hits Downing St.

By CHARLES A. SMITH, International News Service Staff Correspondent.

LONDON, Sept. 13. — King George and Queen Elizabeth escaped injury today when bombs crashed on Buckingham Palace during a terrific four - hour and ten - minute raid by German planes.

Downing Street, where the official residence of Prime Minister Winston Churchill is located, also was attacked.

Incendiary bombs fell in the famous old street, some landing near the doorway of Number 10, but no damage was caused.

An official statement disclosed that a number of civilians were killed and injured in the furious attack.

The private chapel of the Palace, where the sovereigns have retired to pray for victory almost daily since the war began, was completely wrecked.

FALL IN QUADRANGLE.

Investigation showed the damage was heavy—far exceeding that caused on Tuesday when a delayed-action bomb went off just beyond the north wall of the Palace, shattering scores of win-

VICTORIA MEMORIAL.

Two fell in the inner quadrangle, apparently doing small damage.

A third crashed into the chapel, sanctuary of Britain's monarchs since Queen Victoria established Buckingham Palace as the Royal residence a century ago.

The other two fell in the road-

Continued on Page 2, Column 4.

dows and cracking the swimming pool where Princess Elizabeth and Princess Margaret Rose bathed each morning.

Five bombs hit the Palace and its spacious grounds today.

DAILY MIRROR, Wednesday, August 26, 1942.

Daily Mirror

AUG. 26

No. 12,075   ONE PENNY
Registered at the G.P.O. as a Newspaper.

Great Pacific sea-air battle

FROM JOHN WALTERS

NEW YORK, Tuesday.

THE power of the United States and Japanese naval and air forces are to-night locked in a great battle off the Solomon Islands.

Japanese warships, including aircraft carriers, appeared from their bases last Sunday in a desperate attempt to drive the victorious American Marines from the islands.

The Americans met the challenge head-on and so far more than eight of Japan's warships have been damaged, and at least twenty-one of her planes shot down.

But tonight the Japanese are still fighting violently, apparently hoping to crash through the American sea barriers and attack from the rear the U.S. Marines who are now mopping up Japanese garrisons.

In First Phase

The future of the entire Solomons campaign depends on this battle.

Among the Japanese vessels already bombed by Flying Fortresses and planes from American aircraft-carriers are:

One battleship;
Two aircraft-carriers;
Three (at least) fair-sized cruisers;
One transport; and
Several smaller cruisers.

American losses are so far described as "minor ones."

In the first phase of the attack on Sunday, Japanese carriers sent an air fleet to blitz the island of Guadalcanal.

American fighter planes were ready and quickly routed the Japanese, bringing down 21 of their planes.

Then Japanese destroyers shelled Guadalcanal, apparently without doing severe damage.

Following this the enemy fleet approached from the North-East. American land-based Flying Fortresses as well as aircraft-carrier planes went to attack it.

"Great Risks"

The Japanese aircraft - carriers damaged were a big one, disabled by four hits, and the 7,100 - ton Ryuzyo, carrying 24 planes, which was severely battered.

A U.S. Navy spokesman in Washington said tonight that the Japanese were taking great risks to regain a foothold in the important Tulagi area—the main Solomons base. He was confident they would be frustrated.

A previous attempt to dislodge the Americans from the Solomons was made last Thursday when 700 Japanese tried to land near the U.S. Marines' positions from speedboats.

DUKE OF KENT DIES IN CRASH FLYING TO ICELAND

The Air Ministry regrets to announce that Air Commodore the Duke of Kent was killed on active service yesterday afternoon when a Sunderland flying-boat crashed in the North of Scotland.

His Royal Highness, who was attached to the staff of the Inspector-General of the Royal Air Force was proceeding to Iceland on duty.

All the crew of the flying-boat also lost their lives.

This tragic news was announced by the Air Ministry shortly before midnight.

The youngest brother of the King, the Duke, who was in his fortieth year, had been closely associated with the RAF since early in the war.

He was probably the most air-minded member of the Royal Family and its first member to fly the Atlantic. He had flown thousands of miles under war conditions in a plane equipped for battle with enemy aircraft.

For some time he had been making extensive but little-publicised air trips as a means of speedy transit.

The Duke relinquished the honorary rank of Air Vice-Marshal in 1940 when he joined the RAF, so that he should not be senior to experienced officers with whom he had to work in his capacity of welfare officer.

It was in July last year that he made a secret flight to Canada in a Liberator bomber to inspect the Empire air training schools. The crossing took eight hours.

He first landed at Montreal and then flew on to Ottawa in another plane.

Previous Mishap

During the flight the Duke, who held a pilot's licence, spent part of the time in the cockpit.

The Duke learned to pilot a machine in 1930, and lost none of his enthusiasm for flying when he was involved in a plane mishap at Dyce Aerodrome, Aberdeen, in July, 1939.

Wing-Commander Fielden was taxi-ing the machine across the field and increasing speed before lifting when one of the wheels became bogged.

The plane spun round, seemed likely to capsize, then suddenly stopped. The Duke stepped out of the plane, lit a cigarette, and smiled at the adventure.

Since that experience he had flown to various RAF stations and training fields all over the country.

The Duke's last public

Continued on Back Page

One of the last pictures taken of His Royal Highness the Duke of Kent at the christening of his infant son Prince George on August 4. With the Duke and Duchess are their other two children Prince Edward and Princess Alexandra.

The Daily Sketch

SOUVENIR EDITION

No. 11,224   WEDNESDAY, MAY 9, 1945   A KEMSLEY NEWSPAPER   ONE PENNY

THEY SHARED OUR ORDEALS NOW THEY REJOICE WITH US

From a balcony at Buckingham Palace the King and Queen, accompanied by Princess Elizabeth (left) and Princess Margaret (right), smile and wave at the cheering crowd; many thousands strong. (The King's broadcast is on Page 3.)

AFTER THE SURRENDER

On Monday, May 7, at 2.41 a.m., Germany surrendered unconditionally to the Allies at Rheims. Colonel-General Gustav Jodl, the new German Army Chief of Staff, signed for Germany, and General Bedell Smith for the Supreme Allied Command. In the smiling group above, taken after the signing, are (front row) Col. Zikovitch (Russia), Gen. Suslaparov (Russia), Gen. Bedell Smith (U.S.A.), Gen. Eisenhower, Air Chief Marshal Tedder (U.K.), Admiral Burrough (U.K.), Gen. Spaatz (U.S.A.), and Gen. Sevez (France).

Monty Says: 'Now Win The Peace'

"WE have won the German war. Let us now win the peace," said Field-Marshal Montgomery in a personal victory message issued last night to all ranks under his command.

"We all have a feeling of great joy and thankfulness that we have been preserved to see this day," said the message. "We must remember to give the praise and thankfulness where it is due. ' This is the Lord's doing, and it is marvellous in our eyes.'

"Let us never forget what we owe to our Russian and American Allies. This great Allied team has achieved much in war. May it achieve even more in peace.

"Without doubt, great problems lie ahead. The world will not recover quickly from the upheaval that has taken place. There is much work for each of us.

"It may be some difficult times lie ahead for our country, for each one of us personally.

"If it happens, then our discipline will pull us through. But we must

Turn to Back Page, Col. 1

TIMELY WORDS OF FAITH

Praise the Lord, all ye nations: praise him, all ye people. For his merciful kindness is great toward us. . . . Praise ye the Lord.

Psalms, 117, 1-2.

June 9, 1946

Sunday Pictorial

No. 1,630   Twopence

All the Great Pictures:
SOUVENIR NUMBER

VICTORY SPECIAL.

The moment that symbolises the pride of a nation. The King—with the Queen and Queen Mary—takes the Salute as the proud might of Empire passes by.

DAILY GRAPHIC
and Daily Sketch

FRIDAY, JANUARY 31, 1947 ★★★ A KEMSLEY NEWSPAPER FOUNDED IN 1890 1d.

Britain Says Bon Voyage

Royal Family Leave For South Africa To-day

*T*HE King and Queen, with Princess Elizabeth and Princess Margaret, leave London to-day on the first stage of their journey to South Africa.

Owing to the wintry weather, the semi-state drive has been cancelled and the Royal party will travel to Waterloo by car, leaving the Palace at 2.20 p.m.

The heartfelt good wishes of millions will go with the Royal Family on their way south. Across thousands of miles, this journey will be followed by the people of Britain as closely as by the people of the Union of South Africa. The next three months will live in the history of the Commonwealth.

PICTURE GUIDE TO ROYAL TOUR ON MIDDLE PAGES

DAILY GRAPHIC

and DAILY SKETCH

TUESDAY, APRIL 27, 1948 ★★★ A Kemsley Newspaper 1d.

Supremely happy years of marriage

THE KING

in his broadcast speech last night

This has been a memorable and a very happy day for the Queen and me. Apart from its deep significance to ourselves as man and wife, it has been made the occasion of a world-wide expression of kindly goodwill towards us which has greatly moved us. It has been an unforgettable experience to realise how many thousands of people there are in this world who wish to join in the thankfulness we feel for the 25 years of supremely happy married life which have been granted to us.

Looking back over those years, nobody can deny that they have been for all of us who have lived through them, full of difficulty, of anxiety, and often of sorrow.

On me, in my endeavour to fulfil my appointed task, they have laid a heavy burden. I make no secret of the fact that there have been times when it would have been almost too heavy but for the strength and comfort which I have always found in my home.

And so I can find no better way of showing my gratitude to all of you whose good wishes have gladdened us to-day than by wishing you in turn a full share of the happiness with which I have myself been blessed. If you are already happily married, may you long enjoy your life together; and if marriage still lies before you, may it fulfil all your brightest hopes.

Security of home

THE QUEEN

in her broadcast, said

I would like to add to the King's my own words of gratitude.

I, too, am deeply thankful for our 25 years of happiness together, for the opportunities we have been given of service to our beloved country and for the blessings of our home and children.

The world of our day is longing to find the secret of community, and all married lives are, in a sense, communities in miniature.

There must be many who feel as we do that the sanctities of married life are in some way the highest form of human fellowship, affording a rock-like foundation on which all the best in the life of the nation is built.

Looking back over the last 25 years, and to my own happy childhood, I realise more and more the wonderful sense of security and happiness which comes from a loved home.

Therefore at this time my heart goes out to all those who are living in uncongenial surroundings, and who are longing for the time when they will have a home of their own.

I am sure that patience, tolerance and love will help them to keep their faith undimmed and their courage undaunted when things seem difficult.

This morning we felt the moving service in St. Paul's to be one of re-dedication as well as thanksgiving; and I pray that by God's guidance we may have many opportunities of service towards the lands and people we love so well.

Silver Wedding Day: They Kneel in Thanksgiving

TWO kneeling figures a little apart from a mighty congregation, the King and Queen bowed their heads in thanksgiving and prayer at the service in St. Paul's Cathedral, which marked their Silver Wedding yesterday.

Behind them were the members of their family, the Ambassadors of the world, representatives of the Empire and the leaders of the nation. Nearly four thousand people were present on this morning of Royal rejoicing.

The crimson-and-gilt chairs for the King and Queen were set at the foot of the steps leading to the choir. They looked dwarfed under the immensity of the Cathedral dome. But, as the service ran its length, those chairs were the focal point in the thoughts of millions.

Outside were the crowds that had cheered the King and Queen all the way from Buckingham Palace to St. Paul's and would cheer them again and again on the return journey and on the evening drive.

For, as the Archbishop of Canterbury said, "the national celebration of this Silver Wedding Day is in very truth a great domestic festival for us all."

More Silver Wedding pictures on Pages 4, 5 and 8.

Evening Standard

39.733   WEDNESDAY, FEBRUARY 6, 1952   ● Three-halfpence

THE KING DIES IN HIS SLEEP

A peaceful end this morning

The Evening Standard announces with deep regret that the King died early this morning.

The announcement came from Sandringham at 10.45 a.m. It said: "The King, who retired to rest last night in his usual health, passed peacefully away in his sleep early this morning."

With him at Sandringham were the Queen, Princess Margaret and the King's grandchildren, Prince Charles and Princess Anne.

The King was 56. It is 136 days since the operation on his lung. Yesterday he was out rabbit shooting for several hours. To everybody he appeared to be in the very best of health.

To-day he had planned to go out shooting hares. But when game-keepers went to Sandringham House for instructions they were told: "The shoot is cancelled."

One doctor was called to Sandringham before the announcement of the King's death was made. He was 37-year-old Dr. James Ansell, local man who held the title of Surgeon Apothecary to the Sandringham Household.

News of her father's death was telephoned to the new Sovereign in Africa. At once she decided to fly home immediately.

She will arrive at 4.30 p.m. to-morrow and will meet the Privy Council to give orders for Court mourning and the funeral.

By then she will have been proclaimed Queen—at an Accession Council at St. James's Palace at five o'clock this evening.

One of the first outside Sandringham House to hear of the King's death was Queen Mary. The news was telephoned to her at Marlborough House.

She last saw the King on Thursday when she went to tea at Buckingham Palace.

Queen Marie of Yugoslavia went to comfort

◆ **Back Page. Col. One**

This is the picture that first told the people of Britain that all was not well with the King. It was taken on May 3 last year, when the King was driving back to Buckingham Palace after the Festival of Britain dedication service at St. Paul's.

THE NEW QUEEN FLYING HOME

From EVELYN IRONS

NYERI, Wednesday.—The new Queen Elizabeth is flying back to London immediately. She did not hear the news until 45 minutes after the announcement from Sandringham. Her aircraft will arrive in London at 4.30 p.m. to-morrow.

She was told of her father's death as she was driving happily back to the Royal Lodge from a visit to the Tree-Tops estate.

Said a member of her household: "She stood it very bravely, like a Queen."

The news was telephoned to the Royal Lodge by a Nairobi newspaper.

It was decided to withhold it from the new Queen until direct confirmation was obtained from Buckingham Palace.

Then Lieut. - commander Michael Parker, Prince Philip's equerry, broke the news.

Palace call

Soon afterwards a direct radio - telephone call came through from the Royal Family.

The call was routed to the new Queen through a little country post office in the Kenya countryside.

It took nearly 30 minutes for the call to be properly connected and established from London so that the new Queen could receive it.

Brief talk

After she took the call, there followed a brief conversation with Prince Philip—and the decision to leave immediately for Nairobi to

● **Page Two, Col. Four**

The lying in state

AT WESTMINSTER HALL NEXT WEEK

The body of the King will be taken to Westminster Hall, probably this week-end. He will lie in state on a catafalque in the centre of the hall throughout next week, beginning on Monday.

A guard will be maintained night and day.

The funeral is expected to take place early in the following week.

Parliament will be adjourned until after the funeral and will probably be up for ten days or a fortnight.

Duke of Windsor phones Palace

'Profoundly shocked'

NEW YORK, Wednesday.—A statement issued here on behalf of the Duke of Windsor, said: "The Duke and Duchess of Windsor are profoundly shocked by the news of the King's death."

The Duke and Duchess received the news at their hotel.

The Duke telephoned Buckingham Palace this morning.

His secretary said she did not know whether the Duke would fly to England.—BUP.

Two by-elections

They will go on

The King's death does not affect to-day's two by-elections. They are at Southport and Bournemouth East

ONE PROGRAMME ON BBC AND ALL SHOWS CLOSE

Shops clear gay windows

The announcement of the King's death was made on the BBC at 11.15 a.m. Announcer John Snagge added: "The BBC offers profound sympathy to her Majesty the Queen and the Royal Family."

Then the BBC closed down for the rest of the day except for news, special bulletins, shipping forecasts and gale warnings.

The Home and Light programes are to merge until after the funeral. To-morrow serious music will be broadcast on all stations.

On Friday some other suitable programmes may be broadcast. The Third Programm may broadcast independently before the funeral, but a single programme will

be sent out for the next two days.

The overseas broadcasts will give serious music for the next 24 hours, with news and special bulletins. Programmes go back to normal after the funeral.

The television service announced the news then closed on the demonstration film at 11.33 a.m.

At 11.45 screens showed the BBC coat of arms with the announcement of the King's death by the presentation

▲ **Page Two, Col. Three**

WEATHER—Cloudy

Forecast for to-morrow: Moderate S.W. to W. winds; mainly fine, but possibly cloudy at first, with a little rain or drizzle. Further Outlook: Probably fine. Lighting-up time (London) 5.27 p.m.

Daily Mirror

TUES FEB. 12 1952

FORWARD WITH THE PEOPLE

1½d

No. 15,007

Registered at G.P.O. as a Newspaper.

A sorrowing family group of three Queens—Elizabeth the Second, Queen Mary and the Queen Mother—stand at the entrance to Westminster Hall as the King's coffin is carried past them to the Lying-in-State. On the right is Princess Margaret.

CHAPTER 5

ELIZABETH II

Churchill led a chorus of voices hailing a new Elizabethan age.

Elizabeth II was just 25 years old when she inherited her father's throne. The news that King George VI had died in his sleep at Sandringham was broken to Elizabeth by her husband, Prince Philip, on a game reserve in Kenya. She had left Britain a princess, and flew home its Queen — loyally greeted at London Airport by a solemn array of national leaders.

Her Prime Minister, Churchill, at first worried whether she could cope. But he was soon entranced by this dignified and mature young woman, and led a chorus of voices hailing a new Elizabethan age. When the news of the British conquest of Everest coincided with her Coronation day in 1953, it seemed to signal the end of the gloomy post-war era and the beginnings of a new future for Britain.

The Queen's grandmother, Queen Mary, had died just two months before. But the new reign was symbolised by its youth — not just that of the sovereign, but of the new heir to the throne, 3-year-old Prince Charles, whose toys alone were worth a two-page picture feature in the *Daily Graphic*.

1953's Coronation Specials were to prove but a prelude to the reign's first major problem — the love of the Queen's younger sister for a dashing — but divorced — young courtier.

This drama of thwarted Royal romance dominated the newspapers in late 1955 (pp.78-79). Finally Princess Margaret reached her own agonised decision to put her duty before her love, and renounce Group Captain Peter Townsend. The nation's collective heart — for once the newspaper cliché rings true — went out to her.

The changing face of the monarchy during Elizabeth II's reign is marked by the fact that in 1955 she had to dissuade her sister from marrying a divorced man, but 25 years later permitted her to divorce the man she married instead (p.100). Another was the increasingly informal nature of Royal photographs and TV films. The Queen was consciously inching the institution of monarchy closer to its people — while taking care to preserve the essential gulf between the two, without which the mystique of the monarchy would founder.

The late 1950s saw the Queen score great personal triumphs abroad while occasional hiccups continued back home. Lord Altrincham's famous attack on her staff and her vowel sounds earned him a public slap in the face; similar outrage was to greet Malcolm Muggeridge and the playwright John Osborne when they too launched mild criticisms of the monarchy.

For the Queen could do no wrong in the public eye, especially when she gave both public and press morale a great boost by deciding to have more children, with the arrival in 1960 of Prince Andrew (p.84) followed four years later by that of Prince Edward. The years between provided no fewer than three Royal weddings for the newspapers to exult in, not least because all involved "commoners": those of Princess Margaret to Tony Armstrong-Jones, the Duke of Kent to Katharine Worsley and Princess Alexandra to Angus Ogilvy (pp.88).

The Queen's Consort began to exert his own now familiarly independent spirit, most famously in the "Pull Your Finger Out" speech to British industry in 1961. Family ups and downs continued: the Queen's cousin, Lord Harewood had divorced, the much-loved Princess Marina died, and Prince William of Gloucester was killed in an air crash.

But a new peak in the monarchy's popularity was reached in 1969 with the investiture of Prince Charles at Caernarvon — and thus the launch into public life of one of its most popular new figures (p.119). As if inspired by an instinct for public relations, the monarchy continued to offer the press regular crests to the Royal wave: the Queen's and Prince Philip's silver wedding anniversary in 1972, Princess Anne's wedding (again to a commoner) in 1973, the Queen Mother's 75th birthday in 1975, the Queen's 50th the following year, and her triumphant Silver Jubilee in 1977.

Shadows again fell with Princess Margaret's divorce and the murder by Irish terrorists of the Royal Family's favourite uncle, Lord Mountbatten. Blanks were shot at the Queen, who also had to endure an intruder in her bedroom and a sex scandal involving her private detective. But both senior and junior generations were continuing the flow of good news. In 1980 the nation celebrated the Queen Mother's 80th birthday, and in 1982 Prince Andrew's return from the Falklands War provided one of the great Royal photos of all time (p.110).

But the previous year, the entire Royal scene had been single-handedly rejuvenated by a shy 19-year-old called Lady Diana Spencer.

DAILY SKETCH, TUESDAY, APRIL 9, 1935

EXCLUSIVE—THE LIFE OF QUEEN MARY

WIRELESS : P. 26

DAILY SKETCH

SHORT STORY EVERY DAY

No. 8,097   [Registered as a newspaper.]   TUESDAY, APRIL 9, 1935   ONE PENNY

OUT FOR RIDE WITH UNCLE

PRINCESS ELIZABETH ENJOYING A CANTER IN WINDSOR PARK

When staying at Windsor Princess Elizabeth enjoys nothing so much as riding on her pony in Windsor Great Park. Above she is seen with her uncle, the Duke of Gloucester, and Mr. Owen, her riding master, out for a canter in the sunshine. The little Princess has a naturally good seat and wonderful " hands " for one so young. Another picture on page 12.

THE DUKE OF KENT AS BEST MAN: *Pictures, Page 14*

DAILY SKETCH

THE PRINCESSES 4 PICTURE PAGES

No. 8,501   TUESDAY, JULY 28, 1936   ONE PENNY

THE ROYAL DOG LOVERS

Of the delightful series of pictures which the "Daily Sketch" publishes to-day of Princess Elizabeth and Princess Margaret Rose with their parents and their favourite dogs, this one will be treasured for its happy informality. The little princesses with Jane, their three-year-old Corgi, are photographed at Windsor. This picture and others on pages 7, 12 and 17 were specially taken for Major Mitford Brice, and appear exclusively in the "Daily Sketch" to-day and to-morrow.

DAILY GRAPHIC

and DAILY SKETCH

THURSDAY, JULY 10, 1947 ★★★ A KEMSLEY NEWSPAPER   1d.

The King and Queen Announce Betrothal of Their 'Dearly Beloved Daughter': Wedding To Be Soon

ELIZABETH AND PHILIP — Official

THE KING last night made the long-anticipated announcement of the engagement of Princess Elizabeth to Lieut. Philip Mountbatten.

A special Court Circular issued from Buckingham Palace gave the news. It read:

"It is with the greatest pleasure that the King and Queen announce the betrothal of their dearly beloved daughter, Princess Elizabeth, to Lieut. Philip Mountbatten, R.N., son of the late Prince Andrew of Greece and Princess Andrew (Princess Alice of Battenberg) to which union the King has gladly given his consent."

Princess Elizabeth is 21, and Lieut. Mountbatten is 26.

Although the date has yet to be fixed, it is officially stated that the wedding will take place "before next Spring." It is almost certain to take place in Westminster Abbey.

Three-Stone Ring

Lieut. Mountbatten visited Buckingham Palace shortly before the Court Circular was issued. He had motored up from H.M.S. Royal Arthur, a naval training station at Corsham (Wilts), where he has been an instructor since last October.

He dined at the Palace, where he stayed overnight, but Princess Elizabeth was not present.

She had left earlier in the evening, cheered by the waiting crowds, to attend a private dinner party at the Dorchester Hotel, Park-lane.

She did not wear her engagement ring—which is of diamonds and platinum, one large diamond being flanked by two smaller stones set as baguettes.

Afterwards she went on to a dance at Apsley House, Hyde Park Corner, home of the Duke of Wellington.

She was one of the first to arrive and as she stood near her host and hostess—the Hon. Robert and Lady Serena James—as they welcomed the guests, she received many congratulations.

Lieut. Mountbatten's absence was explained by the fact that the engage-

Turn to Back Page, Col. 1

'A MARRIAGE HAS BEEN ARRANGED'—SEE PAGES SIX AND SEVEN

"Daily Graphic" picture last night of Princess Elizabeth arriving at Apsley House for the ball given by Colonel the Hon. Robert and Lady Serena James.

LATE EXTRA

Evening Chronicle

No. 22,313. 1½d. Newcastle. THURSDAY, NOVEMBER 20, 1947. A KEMSLEY NEWSPAPER

This Happy Day

RADIANT PRINCESS WEDS HER SAILOR DUKE

Princess Elizabeth

H.R.H. the Duke of Edinburgh.

Historic Pageant Grips World

HAND-IN-HAND TO MEET RAPTUROUS CROWDS

Princess Elizabeth, the elder daughter of King George VI and Queen Elizabeth, drove in a glittering cavalcade of British pageantry to Westminster Abbey, to-day and was married to H.R.H. the Duke of Edinburgh, as Lieutenant Philip Mountbatten, R.N., is now styled.

THE historic Abbey glowed with colour and beauty, enriched by music, as the radiant Princess solemnly exchanged marriage vows with her sailor 'groom. She promised to "Love, cherish and obey," speaking in a firm, low voice. She looked exquisitely beautiful in a gown like a mist of ivory satin gleaming with a myriad of pearls and crystals. She left the Abbey hand in hand with her husband.

BRIDE WAS POISED AND COMPOSED

By Our Own Special Representative in the Abbey.

The supreme moment is here. For three-quarters of an hour, while the Kings and Queens and great ones of the earth have assembled in pomp and splendour, the organ has filled the Abbey with joyful stirring music.

Now, suddenly, the music stops. For a minute, there is tense silence, heightened for those of us in the Abbey by the pealing of the bells of St. Margaret's and the muffled thunder of an unseen, cheering multitude.

Her Royal Highness the bride

We, near the high altar, know what the silence means. Her Royal Highness the Bride is here. Already, at the great West door beyond our sight, the final touches are being added to the Royal veil and train and bouquet.

As dramatically as the silence came, it ends. From behind and above the high altar a silver fanfare sounds — the thrilling notes which summon Princess Elizabeth forward down the Abbey nave to the altar, ablaze with all the gold plate from the Abbey's treasure chest.

Now, through the noble arch of the choir screen, half-way along the nave, we can see at last the head of the bridal procession.

Fanfare ends

As the fanfare ends we get the first glimpse of Princess Elizabeth on the arm of her father, the King.

She is pale but perfectly poised and composed. The official phrase—" supported by His Majesty "—is indeed but a figure of clerical speech.

Every eye is focussed on her as she comes slowly and superbly to the Lantern—and so intent is that regard that few, I imagine, notice the Duke slip from his oaken pew below the sanctuary and stand waiting to greet her.

Welcoming smile

But now everybody suddenly notices he is there and sees, too, the tender, brief welcoming smile he has for his Royal bride. The smile is returned in an upward glance of happy recognition.

Royalty and splendour are momentarily forgotten as first the Dean and then the Archbishop of Canterbury speak of "this man" and "this woman" and as the clearly heard responses reach our ears from "Philip" and "Elizabeth Alexandra Mary."

The bride and groom kneel for the prayers. At last the Archbishop's words "let no man put asunder" tell the world that the Royal wedding is over.

Tense wait

There is yet another tense wait as the Royal couple disappear into the chapel of Edward the Confessor to sign the register

As the Royal pair come into view and move, radiantly smiling, to their place in the Procession of the Bride and Bridegroom, the organ crashes out into Mendelssohn's "Wedding March." A splendid page of British history turns.

Six Kings and seven Queens attended the wedding, and many other famous personalities. With them in spirit was an unseen audience of millions of people throughout the world, who listened in on the radio to the broadcast descriptions of the ceremonies and added their wishes for the joy and happiness of the bridal pair. The weather was warm, spring-like, but dull after overnight drizzle.

Cabinet Ministers, Empire statesmen, diplomats, peers and commoners and their ladies were at the Abbey, and the sparkling jewellery, beautiful dresses and magnificent uniforms of about three thousand guests presented an unforgettable scene.

Tremendous cheering crowds, many of whom had waited all night in drizzling rain, lined the routes of the five processions to the Abbey. The Duke of Edinburgh and his best man, the Marquess of Milford Haven, arrived by car at the Poet's Corner door just before the King and the Princess left the Palace in the big Irish coach. At the Palace the crowd broke through the police barriers. The Princess entered the Abbey on her father's arm.

The Queen, in a gown of apricot and gold, drove in the glass coach with Princess Margaret, one of the eight bridesmaids, who were all in white. The pages were Prince William of Gloucester and Prince Michael of Kent.

GREAT WELCOME

After the ceremony, the Royal bride and her handsome husband entered the glass coach and received a rapturous reception from the crowds as they drove with the bridal party to Buckingham Palace. The Princess was smiling and waving her hand, while the Duke saluted.

During the Palace reception the crowd broke into the forecourt and mounted police had to be called. In response to the clamour of the throning mass the bride and bridegroom appeared on the balcony and waved to them.

THE WORLD WAS AT WESTMINSTER

By R. K. GERRIE

The whole world was taken to the High Altar of Westminster Abbey to-day. Hearts surged, blood tingled, and there was a lump in the throat of all who were guests of the B.B.C. during to-day's historic broadcast.

WE, the people of the British Empire, shared the happiness of a young woman and a young man. The radio brought the wedding into our homes.

Every fireside became an altar and there were silver shoes on the feet of every woman who left her dinner uncooked to listen to the broadcast.

Never in history has a young bride had such universal affection as went out from the hearts of all who stood with her by the side of the man who is now her husband.

A million marriages were re-lived during those moments when Royalty and commoners were linked by the vows of the Book of Common Prayer. Who will ever forget those living highlights of history, brought to us from the heart of the Empire and recorded for ever?

The first glimpse of the bride departing for the last time as a single woman from the home of her parents, on her way to marry the man she loves.

The voice of the people. The bells. The "ethereal" dress. The bands and the cheers. The Princess's nervous pause as she entered the Abbey.

The responses

The bridegroom's rich firm responses. The slight slip he made in saying ".. till death do us part" instead of ".. till death us do part."

The Princess's own responses ... light, audible, but making us all feel that lump rise in our throats.

At 11.44 a.m. the Royal bride and bridegroom became husband and wife .... and our rejoicing hearts swelled and swelled.

The tension eased with sigh from a million breasts, and we people of the Empire sent out love to the man and girl who have captured it by their own devotion.

Wedding Reports on Inside Pages

The scene in Westminster Abbey—Page 4.

Wedding route scenes—Page 3

The Archbishop of York's address to the Royal bride and her 'groom—Page 2.

Honeymoon Town—Page 2.

Merioneth's Bells of Joy

Merioneth, the earldom of which has been revived after many centuries by the conferment of the title on H.R.H. the Duke of Edinburgh, pealed church bells to-day. The following personal telegram was sent to the Duke by Ald. Griffith, chairman of the County Council:

" The people of Merioneth are delighted at the great honour bestowed on them by the conferment on your Royal Highness of the Earldom of our county, and we look forward to the day when the Princess and yourself will be able to honour us with a visit. Warmest wishes for life-long happiness to you both."

Thursday, November 20, 1947

THE STAR

No 18 530   One Penny

LATE NIGHT

Palace Crowds Break Cordon
After The Wedding And Shout
"THE BRIDE"

Princess Elizabeth, after her marriage to the Duke of Edinburgh appeared with him on the balcony of Buckingham Palace this afternoon a few minutes after an enormous crowd had broken through the police cordon crying " We want the Bride." Above Princess and her husband on the steps of the Abbey.

Daily Mirror

FRI
FEB. 8
1952

1½d

No. 15,004

FORWARD WITH THE PEOPLE

Registered at G.P.O. as a Newspaper.

THIS IS A VERY TRAGIC HOMECOMING
SAID QUEEN ELIZABETH

This was our girl Queen, Elizabeth, as she drove home to Clarence House yesterday—pale, wearing black, wistful but calm. There were no tears. Indeed, there had been a smile when she stepped from her plane. She told Mr. Churchill: "This is a very tragic homecoming." The bravery behind that smile can be guessed at. She is only twenty-five; she has lost a beloved father.—Other pictures in Centre Pages.

FUNERAL IS ON FRIDAY
Three-day public Lying-in-State

THE King will be buried at St. George's Chapel, Windsor, on Friday, February 15—a week today.

This was announced last night three hours after Queen Elizabeth had returned home from Africa.

The Earl Marshal, the Duke of Norfolk, announced that the Queen had approved the following arrangements:—

MONDAY, February 11.—The Royal coffin will be brought to London by train from Sandringham and will be taken to Westminster Hall for the Lying-in-State.

TUESDAY, WEDNESDAY AND THURSDAY, February 12-14.—Westminster Hall will be open to the public between the hours of 8 a.m. and 10 p.m.

FRIDAY, February 15.—There will be a State funeral procession from Westminster Hall to Paddington Station. From there the coffin will be taken by train to Windsor.

FIRST...A CALL TO HER MOTHER

"DAILY MIRROR" REPORTERS

THE Royal Standard flew from the top of Clarence House last night The Queen was in her own home.

As the flag was broken just after five o'clock the slight figure of the Queen, followed by her husband, hurried from her car into the brightly lit hall.

There she embraced her waiting grandmother, Queen Mary. The next minute the staff telephone operator was calling Sandringham.

A few quiet words with Sir Alan Lascelles, her father's Private Secretary —and then the Queen went to the telephone and spoke to her mother.

That was the moment for which she had been rushed by cars and planes through a whole night and a day.

All through the long dash from Africa she looked the same . . . a slender, straight-shouldered figure, a little pale, though sometimes gravely smiling.

The smile she gave at

Continued on Back Page

THE STAR

No 19,837   Three Halfpence

"MY TASK"

The Queen: 'I Shall Work To Advance The Happiness And Prosperity Of My Peoples'

WITH FULL HERALDIC SPLENDOUR

The Garter King of Arms, Sir George Bellew, making the Proclamation of Accession today. On his left was the Duke of Norfolk and, at back, Lord Halifax. (More pictures on Pages 3, 6, 7 and 12.)

PROCLAMATION SHOUT

'Long Live The Queen'

" Star" Reporter

HUGE crowds heard the Queen proclaimed today " with one voice and consent of tongue and heart " as Queen Elizabeth the Second of England.

The proclamation was read first at St James's Palace, where guardsmen mounted a shoulder to shoulder guard opposite Friary Court.

On the forecourt of the Palace stood the Grenadier Guards' band with the colours draped with black.

The drum and fife section of the band stood in Marlborough-road facing the forecourt. The drums were also draped in black.

Prayers At Westminster

It was announced from Westminster Cathedral today that at the evening service on Sunday special prayers will be offered for the Royal Family in their bereavement and for the new Queen.

The First Special

The first Metropolitan special constable to be sworn in to serve the Queen had his warrant card signed by the magistrate, Mr J. L. Pratt, at West London today. He is Mr Lewis Edward Oakman, of Ormiston - grove, Shepherds Bush.

"Radio Times" Supplement

The BBC are printing a free supplement to the "Radio Times" containing revised programmes for February 9-16.

To martial music played by the band of the Grenadier Guards, the Proclamation was read at Charing Cross by the Lancaster Herald, Mr A. G. B. Russell.

God Save The Queen

At the stroke of 11 the Guards sprang to attention and the trumpeters sounded a fanfare.

Then the crowd heard the Garter King of Arms, Sir George Bellew, read the solemn words of the Proclamation, ending with " God Save The Queen."

The Proclamation was made from the first floor balcony on the west side of the square which had a back draping of maroon cloth.

Men bared their heads as the National Anthem was sung.

Flags Raised

As the Proclamation was declared the Union Jacks at halfmast on hundreds of buildings

CONTINUED ON BACK PAGE

FORECAST

Weather forecast for London and SE England until midday tomorrow.

Moderate to fresh NW to N winds. Snow or sleet in places. **Further outlook:** Continuing cold with night frost. Wintry showers.

Lights up 5.30 pm. Sun sets 5 pm, rises tomorrow 7.28 am.

RADIO: Page Five.

QUEEN ELIZABETH MADE THIS DECLARATION TO THE ACCESSION COUNCIL AT ST JAMES'S PALACE TODAY:

Your Royal Highness, my lords, ladies and gentlemen. By the sudden death of my dear father I am called to assume the duties and responsibilities of sovereignty.

At this time of deep sorrow, it is a profound consolation to me to be assured of the sympathy which you and all my peoples feel towards me, to my mother and my sister, and to other members of my family.

My father was our revered and beloved head, as he was of the wider family of his subjects. The grief which his loss brings is shared among us all.

My heart is too full to say more to you today than that I shall always work, as my father did, throughout his reign, to uphold constitutional government and to advance the happiness and prosperity of my peoples—spread as they are all the world over.

I know that in my resolve to follow his shining example of service and devotion, I shall be inspired by the loyalty and affection of those whose Queen I have been called to be and by the counsel of their elected parliaments.

I pray that God will help me to discharge worthily this heavy task that has been laid upon me so early in my life.

New Notes & Coins

Australian Bank officials said today that it would be at least six months before portraits and engraving of Queen Elizabeth would appear on Australian notes and currency. Australia radio reported.

A spokesman said the portraits and engravings would have to be approved by the Queen before the coins were minted.

Premiere Off

The premiere of Cecil B. De Mille's " The Greatest Show On Earth," which was to have been held at the Plaza Theatre next Friday, has been cancelled because of the King's death.

Horticultural Show

Owing to the death of the King it has been decided to cancel the Royal Horticultural Society's show

DAILY GRAPHIC
& DAILY SKETCH

Friday, June 6, 1952   ★★★★★   A Kemsley Newspaper   2d.

The Queen waves from the Palace balcony after the Trooping

16 Pages

All the Royal Pictures

See pages 7, 8, 9 and 10, and read the brilliant account of the TROOPING THE COLOUR ceremony by PAUL GALLICO on Page 6

The "Daily Graphic" is Britain's picture newspaper — you can always SEE the news.

The Queen chooses her seal

This is the seal the Queen will use on State documents and which will also be the pattern for Coronation souvenirs.

★   ★

Haley quits the BBC
Story on Back Page

Tuesday, November 4, 1952

THE STAR

No 20,067   Three Halfpence

Latest Prices—Page Two   LATE NIGHT

Queen Opens Her First Parliament

Prince Charles and Princess Anne—who stood on a chair—joined their parents when the Queen and the Duke of Edinburgh came out on the Palace balcony to wave to the crowds today.

With a smile whose sparkle matched her diamond necklace and tiara the Queen drove to Westminster for today's State Opening of Parliament. Report on Page Three. More pictures on Pages 3, 8 and 9.

SOUVENIR PICTURES

Evening Standard

40,142 TUESDAY, JUNE 2, 1953 Three-halfpence

CORONATION SPECIAL

THE CROWNED QUEEN
Pages of dramatic pictures

The Queen sits in King Edward's Chair wearing the Crown —the supreme moment in the Abbey to-day. On her right is the Bishop of Durham, on her left the Bishop of Bath and Wells. Before her stands the Archbishop of Canterbury.

She drove from Buckingham Palace to Westminster Abbey in her golden coach. Hundreds of thousands cheered her. Beverley Baxter, MP, reports the Abbey ceremony on the Back Page. Page after page of pictures record the dazzling scene.

Daily Mirror

FORWARD WITH THE PEOPLE

1½d No. 15,412 ✦ ✦ ✦ Wednesday, June 3, 1953

CORONATION SOUVENIR

HAPPY

...And this was the happiest picture of all

—AND GLORIOUS

Daily Mirror

FRI AUG. 19 1955

1½d FORWARD WITH THE PEOPLE

No. 16,077

- **The Princess is 25 on Sunday.**
- **Will she wed? When will she announce her decision?**

COME ON MARGARET!

FOR two years the world has buzzed with this question:

Will Princess Margaret marry 40-year-old Group Captain Peter Townsend?—OR Won't she?

Five months ago, Group Captain Townsend told the Daily Mirror: '. . . the word cannot come from me. You will appreciate it must come from other people . . .'

On Sunday the Princess will be 25. She could then, if she wished, notify Parliament direct of her desire to marry without first seeking the consent of her sister the Queen.

She could end the hubbub.

Will she please make up her mind?

Please make up your mind!

Daily Mirror

TUES NOV 1 1955

2^D

FORWARD WITH THE PEOPLE

No. 16,140

MARGARET DECIDES :

DUTY BEFORE LOVE

PRINCESS MARGARET, in this dramatic announcement from Clarence House last night, told the world that she had renounced the love of Peter Townsend:

"I would like it to be known that I have decided not to marry Group Captain Peter Townsend. I have been aware that, subject to my renouncing my rights of succession, it might have been possible for me to contract a civil marriage. But, mindful of the Church's teaching that Christian marriage is indissoluble, and conscious of my duty to the Commonwealth, I have resolved to put these considerations before any others. I have reached this decision entirely alone, and in doing so I have been strengthened by the unfailing support and devotion of Group Captain Townsend. I am deeply grateful for the concern of all those who have constantly prayed for my happiness.

(Signed) Margaret."

Peter Townsend leaves—alone   SEE BACK PAGE

Daily Mirror

THURS OCT 17 1957

2½ FORWARD WITH THE PEOPLE

No. 16,748

Ladies and gentlemen, today the Mirror gives you the loyal toast..

'THE QUEEN!'

Three reforms to make her reign happy and glorious

❶ MORE TRUE LOYALTY

to Her Majesty. The gulf between Palace and People is NOT the fault of the Queen or of Prince Philip.

❷ COMMONSENSE

about the right to criticise as well as to applaud.

❸ SWIFTER CHANGES

In the age of man-made moons, the ghost of Queen Victoria should finally be laid to rest.

YESTERDAY—fresh from her personal triumph in Canada—the Queen began her visit to the United States.

The Mirror acclaims the Queen's achievements in Canada. She delighted everybody by her self-confidence and her warm, human speeches.

It is lamentable that the Queen's brilliant tour abroad should be accompanied by controversy about the Court at home.

The Mirror is angered when personal attacks are made on the Queen. The personality of the Queen should never become involved in argument about the Court.

Some recent criticism went too far. The Queen's voice and appearance should never be the target for ill-mannered comments.

But the Mirror declares that true loyalty to the Queen does NOT mean that all criticism of the Court must be stifled.

Indeed, full loyalty means that such criticisms should be voiced and examined.

If they are justified, then—in the interests of the Queen herself—reforms must follow.

Orders from Above?

The present controversy arises from criticisms of the Monarchy by Mr. Malcolm Muggeridge and Lord Altrincham. It has been fanned into flames by the folly of the B.B.C. in banning both these critics.

General Sir Ian Jacob, Director-General of the B.B.C. **(Better Be Careful),** has turned himself into General Sir " Gag."

Is General Sir " Gag " acting on his own—or has he had orders from above ?

Whatever the answer, this attempt to suppress debate is a blunder and a disservice to the Queen.

It has been alleged that Muggeridge and Altrincham attacked the Monarchy as an institution. That is claptrap.

Both applaud the Monarchy. Both urge reform to make the Monarchy more up to date.

Muggeridge wrote:

" The British Monarch does fulfil an authentic purpose providing a symbolic head of State transcending the politicians who go in and out of office and proving extremely popular with the majority of the people."

Altrincham wrote:

" Those of us who believe that the Monarchy can survive and play an ever more beneficent part in the affairs of the Commonwealth are not content to remain silent while needless errors go uncorrected."

Some people think that the answer to criticism like this is to ignore it.

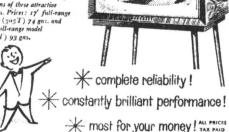

Daily Mirror

TUES
OCT 22
1957

2½

FORWARD WITH THE PEOPLE

✦

No. 16,752

BELLE OF NEW YORK!

MORE than 600,000 wildly cheering Americans hailed the Queen as "Belle of New York" yesterday in a brilliant climax to her American tour.

FULL STORY—Back Page. MORE PICTURES —Centre Pages.

This was how Broadway, New York, looked yesterday as the Queen drove through in a storm of ticker-tape.

Evening Standard

41,796   TUESDAY, OCTOBER 28, 1958   ●● 2½d.

The picture that has never been possible before

INSIDE PARLIAMENT

ONLY 10-PER CENT DOWN ON SOME CARS

Ten per cent down and three years to pay—that was the plan announced by the Standard Car Company at the Motor Show today.

Lord Alexander of Tunis 'seriously ill'

Earl Alexander of Tunis is reported by a Canadian newspaper to be seriously ill with heart trouble in Ottawa.

MCC match drawn

The MCC scored 257 for four in their second innings at Perth today and drew their match with a Combined XI. Cowdrey reached his century in a stand of 166 with Bailey, and Trueman hit a brisk 53.

Mr. Ridge sues

Mr. Charles Ridge, who was acquitted in the Brighton police conspiracy trial, is suing members of the town's watch committee for breach of contract.
For detailed reports see INSIDE PAGES.

A moment of history is recorded by the camera for the first time. The Queen sits on her Throne at Westminster surrounded by all the pomp of her Houses of Parliament and Court.

On her head glitters the Imperial Crown. In her hand is the text of the "Most Gracious Speech" she is reading. For centuries this is a moment that has been zealously guarded from all but those privileged to attend. And, though the camera has existed for more than 100 years, never before has it been allowed to record the splendour of the ceremony of the State Opening of Parliament. — Anne Sharpley's story: PAGE EIGHT.
More pictures : PAGES EIGHT, TEN and ELEVEN

TEN BALLOTS AT VATICAN —NO DECISION

From J. W. M. THOMPSON

ROME, Tuesday. — There was still no Pope this afternoon. Black smoke from the chimney of the Sistine Chapel announced that the cardinals had again failed to elect a successor to Pope Pius XII.

They had two ballots this morning — making ten inconclusive votes.

Jewels stolen

Jewellery worth more than £1000 was stolen from a bedroom at the Stafford Hotel, St. James's Place, during the night.

Nun put on probation

Margaret Elizabeth McMorrow, 40, a nun, was put on probation for two years at Andover today for maliciously setting fire to nine beds at a convent school.

Small-ads. received by 9 p.m. can appear next day.
Ring FLEet Street 3000

WEATHER—Warm—See Page ELEVEN

Daily Mirror

SAT AUG 29 1959

2½ FORWARD WITH THE PEOPLE No. 17,326

HOWDY!

Ike gives a "howdy" wave to the crowds at Balmoral yesterday as the Queen and Duke smilingly look on. Hidden behind the Duke is Princess Margaret. If you look closely you can see one of her shoes and a glimpse of her skirt.

The Queen drives Ike to a picnic

THE Queen drove President Eisenhower to a picnic tea with her children on the shores of Loch Muick, near Balmoral Castle, yesterday.

Ike, who was on a one-day visit to Balmoral, had lunch at the castle.

Soon afterwards he left with the Queen, Princess Margaret, and his son, Major John Eisenhower, on a brief tour of the estate.

The Queen was at the wheel. Later the Duke of Edinburgh took Prince Charles and Princess Anne to meet them at the loch in another car.

Loch Muick is about three miles long and half a mile wide, set in hilly country.

The picnic was at a spot called Glas Allt, where there is a summer-house, now disused, which Queen Victoria used to visit regularly.

"How Nice of You to Meet Me"— SEE CENTRE PAGES

Daily Mirror

ROYAL SOUVENIR ISSUE

Saturday February 20, 1960

2½ ✦ No. 17,474

OH BOY!

Radiant and happy... the Queen pictured when she arrived in London from Sandringham to await the birth of her third child —the new Prince who is now second in line to the Throne.

TWENTY-ONE words thrilled the nation yesterday—the announcement that the Queen had given birth to a son.

It said: "The Queen was safely delivered of a son at 3.30 p.m. today. Her Majesty and the infant Prince are both doing well."

The notice, hung on the railings outside Buckingham Palace, was signed by Mr. John Peel, the gynaecologist, Dr. Vernon Hall, the anaesthetist, and Sir John Weir and Lord Evans, the Queen's physicians.

The baby Prince, whose weight has not yet been announced, is sharing a room with Sister Helen Rowe, adjoining the Queen's room.

A few hours after the birth, the Duke of Edinburgh took Anne to see her new brother.

Later, Prince Charles was given special leave from Cheam School and was driven home to the Palace. Immediately he arrived he, too, saw the baby.

Up and down the country bells rang and flags flew, and from all over the world messages of congratulation poured in to the Palace.

● More news and pictures on
Pages 3, 9, 12, 13 and 24

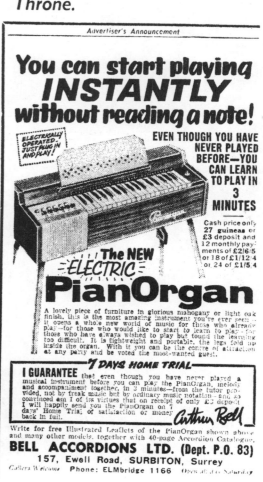

CITY PRICES

FOR BETTER AIR CONDITIONS
IN with **Vent-Axia** **OUT** with
FUG · FUMES · SMELLS and STEAM
60 ROCHESTER ROW · LONDON · S.W.1 · TEL: VIC 2244

Evening Standard

42,267　　FRIDAY, MAY 6, 1960　　●● 2½d.

ROYAL
WEDDING
EDITION

All England here, whose symbol is the Rose, Prays that this Lady's Fortune may be fair

JOHN MASEFIELD TODAY

'Perhaps we had never known how beautiful she is'

By ANNE SHARPLEY

In splendour, sunshine and great sweetness, Princess Margaret married Mr. Antony Armstrong-Jones, the young man without title, without pretension, today in Westminster Abbey.

It was something that could have happened only in the 20th century—a Sovereign's daughter marrying a photographer with all the force of the centuries of this ancient land bringing dignity, grace and deep approval.

Princess Margaret — perhaps we have never known before how beautiful she is — kept a sweet gravity about her that we had never seen.

The simplicity and lightness of her gown, her quiet air. She was a woman surrounded by all the white mystery of womanhood.

Her young husband, Antony Armstrong-Jones, kept looking at her with what seemed to be tender astonishment, as though this was a Margaret he had never seen before.

Only a little earlier, before the Princess went up the aisle he was a little pensive. But he whispered to Dr Roger Gilliatt, his best man, who seemed to be encouraging him.

Together the couple made their vows, she in the light, sweet, steady voice that we know so well: he inexperiencedly in a low, inaudible voice.

But they were brought so close by the moments they were sharing that when they turned their faces seemed momentarily almost the same.

The same small meditative smile, the same downcast eyes.

Around them, close to

▲ Page 14, Column Two

Out of the Abbey they come, man and wife, their hands firmly clasped and looking **completely relaxed and happy.** This was the moment the crowd had been waiting for.

SUNDAY PICTORIAL

June 11, 1961   No. 2,408   © Sunday Pictorial Newspapers, Ltd., 1961   5d.

THE NEWSPAPER FOR THE YOUNG IN HEART

On the Palace balcony...

HRH ANDY CAPS IT ALL

ANDY SHOWS HIS TEETH

... AND THEN HIS TOES

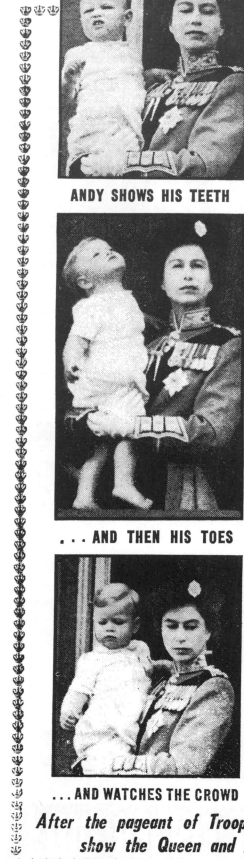

...AND WATCHES THE CROWD

After the pageant of Trooping the Colour in London yesterday, Prince Andrew steals the show! These pictures show the Queen and Andrew on the Palace balcony, watching the RAF fly-past. Story—BACK PAGE

Daily Mirror

3d.   Wednesday, October 18, 1961   ◆   No. 17,989

Prince Philip told Britain yesterday:

PULL YOUR FINGER OUT!

PRINCE Philip made an astonishingly frank remark yesterday to bosses and workers in British industry. He said "I think it is about time we pulled our fingers out."

He was speaking to 120 industrial chiefs at a London lunch. And in a hard-hitting speech, the 40-year-old Prince hammered the workers and bosses who "live in a little world of their own."

The Duke of Edinburgh . . . "I could use several stock phrases," he said. "But I prefer the one I picked up during the last war."

Prince Philip spoke of what he called the most discouraging picture of industry . . .

"It is produced," he said, "by that distressingly large proportion of responsible people in all parts of industry who simply will **NOT** look ahead . . . who don't seem able to profit from past instances, or take advantage of the experience of others."

Ignorant

Prince Philip went on: "They live in a little world of their own, blissfully ignorant that reality has passed them by, until one day they wake up and find themselves ruined.

"When that happens, it is never their fault. Everything and everybody else is to blame. They never suspect their own shortcomings.

"The more they DESERVE criticism, the more they RESENT it."

Prince Philip, husband of the Queen, said that for him "sitting on the fence" was an occupational necessity—but he could claim to be "a reasonably well-informed spectator."

As a spectator, he said, he wanted

WE'RE TOO SLOW TOO SLEEPY

TOO DAMN SMUG!

to see the goose which laid the golden eggs being "cherished and fattened—and not having its neck wrung."

Prince Philip went on "It is not as if we did not know the answer to virtually all the problems of industrial relations.

"It is just that some people are blind and deaf to what can be achieved.

"These people are not deliberately malicious. They are simply **OUT OF TOUCH. . . .**

"Unfortunately, there is no simple and direct way of dealing with these people. . . .

"The bastions of the smug and the stick-in-the-mud can only be toppled by persistent undermining."

Nowadays, Prince Philip warned, a

He hits out at smug industry

◁ THIS is what the Mirror said back in November, 1957. Yesterday, Prince Philip said it again. . . .

nation's reputation abroad could be upheld only by reliability in trade.

"Rocket-rattling does not impress anyone," he said.

"Just at this moment, we are suffering a national defeat comparable to any lost military campaign. And what is more, it is self-inflicted."

Confident

Prince Philip told his audience—all members of the Industrial Co-partnership Association, whose aim is better relations in industry—that he was confident about the "tremendous possibilities" for British industry.

But he made it plain that **FIRST** it is necessary for all concerned to take to heart an expression he picked up as a Royal Navy officer.

"I could use several stock phrases," he said. "But I prefer the one I picked up during the last war."

THAT was the slogan which says—

PULL YOUR FINGER OUT!

DAILY ✦ SKETCH

SOUVENIR EDITION   THURSDAY APRIL 25, 1963 ...... PRICE 3d.

I LOVE YOU...

... whispered the bride to her groom at Westminster Abbey yesterday. The full story of this magic moment is told on Page 9. Also inside—

PAGES AND PAGES OF PICTURES

And best of all —on the Centre Pages— the warm and moving report of

GODFREY WINN

DAILY SKETCH

Wednesday, May 19, 1965   Price Fourpence ★★★   WEATHER: Thunder showers

The Queen appeals to West Germany : Let's be partners in Europe

KAMERADSCHAFT!

(COMRADESHIP)

To dinner in a Rhineland castle. The host last night: West German President Heinrich Luebke. Chief guest: The Queen, wearing a Hardy Amies bell-skirted turquoise gown.

By GEORGE GORDON

NOW let's all pull together. That was the Queen's message to West Germany last night.

THE SETTING: The splendour of Augustusburg Castle in Bruehl, 10 miles north of Bonn. More than 2,500 guests thronged reception rooms ablaze with chandeliers and candles as, outside, German soldiers held flaming torches.

A gasp of admiration went up from hundreds of guests as the Queen descended the staircase on the arm of President Leubke, who had earlier entertained 98 guests to dinner in the apartments above.

The Queen's bell-skirted turquoise satin gown, worn with a white stole and a tiara, echoed the design and colours of the castle decorations.

THE QUEEN said: "We are anxious to play our full part within the European community.

"We must create an atmosphere of mutual confidence between the countries of Europe and a willingness to plan for the future in genuine co-operation.

"Without this, any thought of a genuine European unity will remain a dream."

She went on to say that her presence in Bonn was "testimony to the firm conviction of my Government and people that the important tasks ahead of us can only be solved in the closest co-operation, for which the earlier centuries of friendship provide an encouraging pattern and example today."

A MENTOR...

Earlier President Luebke talked of West Germany's determination to "make up for the past."

He said:

"At a time when Germany was engaged in a long and painful struggle for its political unity, Britain was already a leading nation of the world and a mentor for other nations."

He went on: "Britain and Germany are neighbours whose mutual relationship has over the centuries gone through all the degrees of human and political relations.

"Up to the outbreak of the first war there were hardly any serious conflicts between our two countries. . . ."

Those ties remained unbroken until "the terrible event that took place between 1940 and 1945."

'SIGN OF TRUST'

He then quoted an extract from a speech by Sir Winston Churchill calling for a United States of Europe.

He said: "It is our hope and desire to see Your Majesty's country included in that European Union.

"We also regard your visit as a sign of the growing trust in our people.

"We believe that the

➡ *Back Page*

Germans forbidden to 'heil'

—See Centre Pages

Daily Mail

TUESDAY, AUGUST 29, 1972

3p

The last picture...as William gave his plane a final polish

PILOT PRINCE DIES IN CRASH

Minutes before take-off, the Prince and Mrs Gillian Mitchell, his co-pilot's wife, polish the plane

DID Prince William of Gloucester die because of a piloting error?

That is the question a civil aviation inquiry into yesterday's crash will try to answer today.

The 30 - year - old Prince crashed in his Piper Cherokee Arrow 30 seconds after he took off from Halfpenny

By KEITH COLLING and GARETH PARRY

Green, Staffordshire, in an air race.

The plane banked steeply to the left and hit a tree. The left wing broke off and the rest plummeted 100ft. into a country lane and burst into flames.

One competitor said the Prince was trying to get into the race circuit as quickly as possible. 'It looked as though he banked too low and turned too sharply.'

In a steep turn a plane needs more speed to keep airborne. It may have stalled.

A loss of power in the engine could have had the

same result. This is the main point that crash investigators will try to clear up.

Last night race officials denied there was mechanical failure.

But Mr Simon Ames, a friend of Prince William's and another competitor in the race said : 'He was about 150 feet up when he started his turn. The aircraft seemed to start losing height while in the turn and to have come down until it struck the tree.

'Mechanical failure could have been a factor.'

The Prince and Lieut.-Commander Vyrell Mitchell, who

went along for the ride, were killed instantly.

Commander Mitchell, 43, a sales director of the Piper distributing company lived at Abingdon, Berkshire.

Mr Mitchell's wife, Gillian, mother of two, was among the 33,000 crowd who saw the crash. She was taken from the airfield suffering from shock.

The Prince had piloted Commander and Mrs Mitchell from his home near Peterborough

The Commander, who was in the Fleet Air Arm, taught the Prince most about flying. Together they made a 10,000-mile trip across the world in 1968.

The Prince arrived at

Turn to Page 14, Col. 1

The Queen cancels Olympic visit and orders mourning

THE QUEEN has cancelled her visit to the Olympic Games with Princess Anne, which was due to begin today.

And she ordered family mourning to be observed until Prince William's funeral.

Prince Philip, who is in Munich as an Olympic official, will fly back to Britain for the funeral.

Flags on official buildings throughout the country will

fly at half-mast today and on the day of the funeral.

The Queen heard the news of the Prince's death at Balmoral.

GORDON GREIG writes : A review of the flying activities of the Royal Family, particularly Prince Charles, is certain to be held.

The subject will probably be discussed between the Prime Minister's office and Palace advisers.

But it is doubtful if any restrictions will be made

Daily  Mail

TUESDAY, NOVEMBER 21, 1972

3p

SILVER WEDDING SPECIAL

On a day of mingled joy and pageantry, the Queen pokes fun at her own famous 'catch-phrase'

MY HUSBAND AND I

By DAVID HUGHES

THE Queen took a smiling dig at her own formal speeches yesterday when she rose to her feet in Guildhall.

She said : 'I think everybody really will concede that on this, of all days, I should begin my speech with the words : "My husband and I." '

The sally was greeted by a great roar of laughter and applause that went on for nearly half a minute. Later, to more applause, she went on to recall that a bishop, asked what he thought about sin, once replied : 'I am against it.'

The Queen said : 'If I am asked today what I think about family life after 25 years of marriage I can answer with equal simplicity and conviction. I am for it.'

She was replying to the toast proposed by the Lord Mayor of London, Lord Mais, at the Silver Wedding anniversary luncheon in her honour.

Her remarks caught the spirit of a day when the accent was on humour and informality rather than pomp and circumstance.

The fun continued at the Barbican walkabout which followed the luncheon.

It was one of the greatest royal occasions the City has ever seen with the Queen, Prince Philip, Prince Charles and Princess Anne wandering freely among thousands of ordinary people and pausing to chat when the fancy took them.

'How long have you been married ?' Prince Philip asked one couple.

'Eleven years,' they told him.

'The first 12 years are the worst,' the Prince assured them, grinning cheerfully. 'After that it's all downhill.'

Favourite

During the 45-minute walkabout, City typists shrieked with laughter when Prince Charles asked them : 'Are you the sort of girls who sit on the boss's knee ?'

Princess Anne, in a bright fuchsia coat, was a great favourite. As the confetti rained down from the sky-scraper blocks, seven-year-old Carrie Welsh, of Hendon, called : 'Princess Anne, Princess Anne.'

The Princess came over and Carrie gave her a silver mug with a card attached bearing the inscription : 'To the Queen and Prince Philip.'

The Princess gave it to the Queen.

Earlier, at Westminster Abbey, a fanfare of trumpets heralded the arrival of the Royal Family.

But the service was, in the main, a simple one with the emphasis on the family occasion.

The gaiety continued in the evening, when Prince Charles and Princess Anne gave a party at Buckingham Palace for their parents.

Marriage—by the Queen, Page 2.
Silver Wedding Diary, Page 15.
Royal Walkabout, centre pages.

BEA crash pilot 'had heart trouble'

— PAGE 13

Poulson faces £¼m claim

— PAGE 11

Mountain girl saved

— PAGE 3

PLUS

The glance that bridges 25 years

Picture by Michael Brennan.

Daily Mirror

EUROPE'S BIGGEST DAILY SALE

3p   Thursday, November 15, 1973   ✦   No. 21,720

Her Royal Highness...

MRS PHILLIPS!

✱ In a dark emergency November, a touch of summer for a young Princess

PICTURE: KENT GAVIN

THE INTIMATE PICTURES Souvenir Issue

WEATHER:
Cool.
Lighting-up time:
9.45 p.m. to 4.13 a.m.
Details—Back Page.

46,622

Evening Standard

CITY PRICES

London: Monday June 10 1974   5   4p

At 74—after years confined to a wheelchair:
Gloucester, the last of George V's sons

THE SOLDIER DUKE DIES

THE DUKE OF GLOUCESTER

Jenkins faces storm on IRA

By ARTHUR HAWKEY

HOME SECRETARY Roy Jenkins was preparing today to meet angry protests from Tory backbenchers who are incensed at the freedom with which IRA men openly flaunted their sinister "uniforms" in London during the funeral ceremonial for dead hunger - striker Michael Gaughan at the weekend.

Other questions were expected on just how soon the Home Secretary expects to transfer the Price sisters to Northern Ireland and to what extent other Party leaders have agreed to honour any undertakings that may have been given to the two women.

Mr Jenkins was likely to defend his action on the ground that it is ill-advised to provide the IRA with martyrs to their

Contd. Back Page, Col. 4

● Kidnap: Hunt for renegade Provo—Page 7.

THE NEW DUKE—Prince Richard, 29, with his wife, 27-year-old Princess Richard.

Standard Reporters

THE DUKE of Gloucester died at 12.30 this morning at his home, Barnwell Manor, Northamptonshire. A statement from Kensington Palace said the 74-year-old duke "died peacefully in his sleep."

The duchess was at Barnwell Manor at the time of the duke's death. Prince Richard, 29 —the new duke—was with his wife 27-year-old Princess Richard at Kensington Palace. Princess Richard has been "indisposed" since the beginning of May.

The funeral of the duke, the last of the Queen's uncles and the only surviving child of King George V and Queen Mary, will be at St George's Chapel, Windsor.

Burial at Frogmore

The duke, whose great love was the Army, will be buried at Frogmore. His son Prince William and his brother the Duke of Windsor are buried there.

No date has been set. It will be announced later today from the Lord Chamberlain's Office.

No medical bulletin on the cause of the duke's death had been issued so far, said a Kensington Palace spokesman.

"He has been in failing health as a result of a circulatory complaint for some considerable time. It is just the case that the disease has finally taken its toll."

The duke's condition has been causing anxiety for some days. The closing years of his life were marred by failing health and the deep personal tragedy of the death of his elder son and heir, Prince William, in an air crash in August 1972.

For some years the duke has undertaken no public engagements. He spent much of his time in a wheelchair at Barnwell. The family frequently took him for drives around the estate and into the Northamptonshire countryside.

The 72-year-old duchess who takes an active part in charitable work, carried out public engagements for the duke.

Visit cancelled

Prince Richard has cancelled an engagement to attend the opening in London today of an exhibition to mark 100 years of lawn tennis.

The Queen, who is at Windsor, and Prince Philip—53 today—were informed of the duke's death.

Prince Philip was due to attend the annual court of Trinity House in London and see the 25-year-old Prince of Wales elected an Elder Brother of Trinity House.

Later, Prince Philip was to attend a World Wildlife Fund Press conference and reception. He is president of the British National Appeal.

Duke who did his duty. News on camera—Page 3.

His greatest love.

Page 7

The architect prince succeeds

PRINCE RICHARD, 29, a sensitive, artistic young man and eighth in line of succession to the throne, is the new Duke of Gloucester.

Responsibility as heir to the title came upon him suddenly when his elder brother, 30-year-old Prince William, died in an air crash in August 1972.

Only six weeks had gone by since he was best man at Prince Richard's wedding to the former Danish secretary, Miss Birgitte van Deurs.

The Duke could not attend the wedding. He remained at home in a wheelchair.

Prince Richard has not only carried on with his profession as an architect, but has assumed more and more responsibility for running the Barnwell estate.

He is a partner in a firm of architects. Last year he published a book, The Face of London, and his artistic temperament caused him to write that the City of London was "a bit of a mess."

He wrote: "It has to be a commercial centre, but sooner or later there must be an end. Office blocks are getting so large

Contd. Back Page, Col. 3

Three killed in pile-up

THREE people died and seven were injured in a multiple car crash on the eastern end of the North Circular Road, at Walthamstow.

Firemen with cutting and lifting equipment went to the scene. While they tried to cut away the tangled wreckage, to reach the victims a team of doctors set up an emergency drip feed. Traffic was diverted for several hours.

Two of the dead were named as David Wate, 19, of Cheynes Road, Leytonstone, driver of one of the cars, and his passenger Derek Sowgave, 18, of Badlis Road, Waltham Forest.

The third person killed was a woman passenger in another car.

IN YOUR 56-PAGE STANDARD

Daily Mirror

EUROPE'S BIGGEST DAILY SALE

5p   Monday, August 4, 1975   →   No. 22,245

ON THE OCCASION OF HER SEVENTY-FIFTH BIRTHDAY
(Photographed by PETER SELLERS) BRITAIN'S GREATEST GRANDMOTHER

THE proud grandmother. The Queen Mother and the Prince of Wales pose on the eve of her seventy-fifth birthday for the camera of actor Peter Sellers. In her time Elizabeth Bowes-Lyon has lived through many momentous events. Two world wars, the Blitz, the atom bomb, the Space programmes.

She has seen great kingdoms fall and famous statesmen depart. Now she holds the arm of Prince Charles, the young man who is heir to a thousand years of British history.

Holds it proudly—and with affection.

PLEASE TURN TO PAGE 5

Daily Mirror

EUROPE'S BIGGEST DAILY SALE

6p   Wednesday, April 21, 1976   →   No. 22,465

50 TODAY!

Why Jim couldn't go to the party

By JOHN DESBOROUGH

PREMIER James Callaghan turned down a personal invitation from the Queen to attend her fiftieth birthday party at Windsor Castle last night.

Instead, Mr. Callaghan stayed at his Sussex farm and kept working on his official papers.

A Buckingham Palace spokesman said: "The Prime Minister was invited but was unable to come."

The official reason for his absence was pressure of work. Mr. Callaghan had spent the Easter weekend deep in his official papers and was still "reading himself in" last night at his farm.

Accepted

Now the Queen has invited Mr. Callaghan and his wife Audrey to dinner at Windsor next week. This will give him an opportunity for a long informal chat with her.

There was a swift reaction to any suggestion that Mr. Callaghan might appear to be snubbing the Queen by not going to her birthday party.

"Not true," it was said. The Queen quite understood why he could not attend.

And if there had been the slightest hint of a snub, there would have been no invitation to dinner at Windsor next week.

Among those who accepted invitations were former Prime Minister Harold Wilson and his wife Mary, who had been holidaying in the Scillies over Easter.

And ex-Tory leader Edward Heath flew back from Spain specially for the celebration.

Also there were the present Tory leader Mrs. Margaret Thatcher and her husband, and Liberal leader Jeremy Thorpe and Mrs. Thorpe.

Wonderful

Before the Windsor Castle party there was a private dinner for the royal family and close friends.

A Buckingham Palace spokesman said last night: "Obviously we can only tell it from our point of view. The Callaghans were invited and were not able to go.

Today the 180 holders of the Victoria Cross and the George Cross will go to a special birthday tea with the Queen.

The president of the heroes' association said: "It was entirely her own doing. We thought it was a wonderful thing she should give up half her birthday for us."

From the Mirror's 12,500,000 readers..

At 21 1947, year of her engagement. She told her people: "I'm devoted to your service."

At 50 The Queen today. Her promise is fulfilled. But perhaps too, the strain is showing.

The BEST of British birthdays, Ma'am!

A HAPPY and glorious birthday, Ma'am.

The Mirror toasts your half-century with affection, warmth and pride.

We haven't always seen eye to eye. Particularly over some of the Royal pay rises. But our criticism has never been personal.

Today we would like to be very personal indeed. We think you are the tops. And damned good at your job.

Like Queen Elizabeth I and Queen Victoria, you've shown that being a monarch is something a woman can do every bit as well as any man. And in some cases better.

The monarchy in Britain today is immensely popular. No small thanks to you.

We've had our troubles since your Coronation in 1953. But the status of the monarchy has gone from strength to strength.

Today the Mirror wishes you the best of British birthdays. And many more of them.

ELIZABETH, THIS IS YOUR LIFE—PAGE 9

The New Zealand Herald

Telephones { Classified Advertising - 78-999 / Other Departments - 78-988

AUCKLAND, WEDNESDAY, FEBRUARY 23, 1977 2 Price 10c Air Freight 12c

THAT ROYAL MAGIC RETURNS

Smiles, Cheers Turn Rain Into Sunshine

The old royal tour magic returned to Auckland yesterday.

And the city responded with ready smiles, spontaneous cheers and an eagerness simply to catch a glimpse of the Queen and the Duke of Edinburgh as they began their two-week tour of New Zealand.

The aura almost overcame the informality of a visit which marks the silver jubilee of the Queen's reign.

Traffic jammed, people fainted, some of the lucky ones who spoke to the Queen and Prince Philip got tongue-tied — and thousands just stood in the rain waiting for a sight of royalty.

It was a day for families and a special day for the grandparents and the under-12's.

Showers

And it was a day which — on their own admission — held its share of moments for the royal visitors. The Queen confided that, among other events, she found the official welcoming ceremony, the royal salute and military review at Devonport naval base a notably moving occasion.

The Queen and duke arrived on time at the review area soon after 10 am during one of the many showers that threatened to dampen the whole day.

It rained again as a crowd of nearly 40,000 waited for Her Majesty and Prince Philip to motor down Queen St as far as Shortland St, where they began their "walkabout" to the Downtown centre and a civic luncheon.

However, it was "really worth it" in the view of the thousands who sheltered under two great ribbons of umbrellas along the cordon lines down Queen St.

Long Trip

It was worth it, too, to more than 3000 schoolchildren who dodged showers at Ellerslie racecourse as they waited for their own royal garden party to begin about 3 pm.

It was worth even more to Mr and Mrs G. D. Court, of Vancouver, who came to this country to follow the tour and who hope to chat to the royal couple.

Mrs Court, aged 72, said: "I have spoken to the Queen Mother, Princess Anne and Prince Charles."

The first to show the same enthusiasm for the arrival of the Queen and Prince Philip were the crews of 200 or more boats which welcomed the royal yacht amid choppy seas.

Exhilarating

The exhilarating conditions were matched by the spectacular military pageantry of the Devonport naval base welcome—earlier described modestly by the Navy as a simple ceremony.

From then it was informality.

The Queen, who had mingled with the public along Devonport wharf, alighted from her limousine just above Shortland St in Queen St to an immediate roar of approval, after being driven over the harbour bridge to the city centre.

Already there had been hard luck for some. Ambulance staff had had to treat several people who had fainted while waiting.

What Auckland lacked in bunting, it made up for in people. They stood four and five deep along the rope barriers, and surged in a wall-to-wall mass as the royal couple walked towards Downtown.

To the chagrin of the people on the left, the Queen kept to the right-hand side. The duke, however, dallied up to 50 metres in the rear to chat animatedly to those on the left.

Leisurely

Although few shops closed, every Queen St worker appeared to have managed to see the royal couple.

At the leisurely two-hour civic luncheon for 800 people at Trillo's Downtown reception lounge, which followed the walkabout, New Zealand's race relations and the difference between a hereditary monarchy and an elected president were among the topics at the top table.

A large cheering and flag-waving crowd saw the royal couple leave for the racecourse. In Market Rd, Remuera, bowlers interrupted their game to join schoolchildren and nuns on the pavement.

Excitement

Farther along the street six young cyclists joined the royal cavalcade and tried to provide an outrider escort to Ellerslie. Their bid for fame was stymied several blocks along by the intervention of traffic officers.

At the racecourse, children from 242 schools, relaxed by band music, found themselves in a state of excitement as the Queen and the duke, taking separate courses, circulated among them.

Ten-year-old Russell Tukukino, of Hay Park School, Mt Roskill, was stunned after a brief talk with the Queen.

"I wasn't nervous," he said. "I was petrified. But she was fantastic."

A little more than 45 minutes later 2000 people in Quay St cheered and whistled as the royal party arrived to board the Britannia at Princes Wharf.

Last night the royal couple attended a reception on board Britannia.

Early today the Britannia, with the Queen and duke on board, was steaming towards Whangarei, helped along by 10-to-20-knot south-westerlies in light seas. She was expected to pass a few stragglers in the round-the-North Island yacht race which the duke started yesterday morning.

The Queen meeting senior pupils of St Cuthbert's College and the Diocesan High School for Girls at the gathering of young people at Ellerslie Racecourse yesterday.

Prince Presents Gold Awards

By TED REYNOLDS

For some lucky people, the veranda deck of the royal yacht Britannia was one of the most pleasant places in Auckland yesterday afternoon.

There under a red-and-white-striped canvas awning 80 young people from many parts of the North Island received from Prince Philip the gold award of the Duke of Edinburgh scheme which encourages achievement among teenagers.

Parents, new-frocked and dry-cleaned, squeezed behind the ranks of their young. And, although there was little room to move, fathers who had appointed themselves family photographer quickly established a routine of fairly reverent jostling so that in alphabetical order they could stand up front to get the shot that is destined to be No 1 in the family album.

The recipients themselves curtsied without a stumble or shook hands firmly and immediately on receiving their certificates started moving off briskly but every time were stopped in their tracks by a question from Prince Philip, a quick grin and a remark on what they had done.

Staff Drinks

Then back to their ranks they went, faces tense with smiles that only modesty and or embarrassment prevented from turning into face-cracking grins.

Later, as the sun was beginning to fade, the Queen's New Zealand royal tour staff went on board for drinks with the Queen and Prince Philip.

Just before dinner, on went the press party that is covering the tour. A great number of them there were scattered over Auckland yesterday — mainly from London but there were also Australians, a Swede (who asked at Devonport: "Do you call this weather for ducks?"), two French, and somewhere a German from a magazine that makes its owners rich by reporting that the Queen is having a baby, is resigning, is having a row, has gone broke or is investing all her money in a brewery.

Before the press party went on board, the Queen's press secretary gave us a quick briefing. No one could report what happened but we could write about the atmosphere.

So what was the atmosphere like?

Quick Sip

The party itself was about as unstuffy as could be. The Queen accepted a drink from one of her servants and he must have inquired whether it was to her taste because she took a quick sip and turned it in her mouth while the two of them stood there.

The Queen and the Duke talked, she in a general way, he wanting precise answers to exact questions.

They left us with the impression that each of us had been invited at their special request. And that must be a feat in itself.

The Duke of Edinburgh acknowledging the crowd as he walked down Queen St yesterday.

CHAUFFEUR QUICKLY RECOGNISED

Rolls-Royce chauffeur Mr H. E. "Frosty" Symonds was royally remembered yesterday.

Mr Symonds, a veteran of four previous royal tours, was once again behind the wheel.

And the Queen remembered him.

"Good morning Symonds, it is nice to see you still driving," she said on entering the car.

"Frosty" was "tickled pink" to be so remembered. "She is looking beautiful," he said, "just like a queen."

QUICK CHANGE

The Duke of Edinburgh provided a surprise for the crowd that gathered near Trillo's downtown reception lounge, venue of the civic luncheon, yesterday.

He entered resplendent in the uniform of Admiral of the Fleet and came out two hours later casually dressed in a lounge suit.

The changing process also took many of the 800 guests unawares. The duke was in uniform when he signed the visitors' book but was wearing the suit when he sat down to lunch a few minutes later.

Letter To Queen Paid Off

Miles Roelants, a small boy in a large wheelchair, met a pen friend at Ellerslie yesterday — the Queen.

Three years ago, Miles waited patiently with his mother for the Queen to appear at the Wilson Home.

But a glimpse of royalty eluded the seven-year-old boy.

"Mum got so sick of waiting we drove home," he said yesterday.

Miles wrote to the Queen and complained.

He got a reply, and the normally self-assured young lad admitted: "I nearly fainted."

Yesterday, Miles' patience was rewarded.

Nearly submerged in his wheelchair, he peered up at the Queen as she stopped to talk to a cluster of crippled children.

"I didn't see much of her, but what I saw was pretty good," he said.

He said he liked her smile and her hat.

Miles reckoned the Queen was worth writing to.

Trust to Mark Jubilee Visit

Staff Reporter Wellington

An environmental trust will be set up to commemorate the silver jubilee visit of the Queen to New Zealand.

The Prime Minister, Mr Muldoon, said yesterday that the Government had decided some time ago to establish a national trust to operate in the environmental area to ensure that sufficient "open space" was provided for the needs of all New Zealanders.

It would be known as the Queen Elizabeth II National Trust and would be run by an eight-member board and assisted by six government departments actively involved in the field of open spaces.

Basically the trust's functions would be to protect landscape character and scenic values and provide a variety of recreational opportunities and open space experiences.

Land Review

The trust would also undertake:

- A continuing review of the adequacy and accessibility of all forms of reserve land.
- To classify reserves or potential reserves including recreation areas as of national, regional or local significance.
- To classify areas of special significance which would be given statutory protection, revocable only by Parliament.
- To negotiate conservation covenants, easements and access agreements with willing landowners.
- To identify areas of outstanding natural value and to work with local and regional authorities for their protection and designation.

In addition, Mr Muldoon said, the trust would be given power to purchase or receive, by way of gift or bequest, land or rights over land in its own name.

Membership of the trust would be available to individuals, non-corporate private organisations and corporate bodies.

The funds accumulated, together with government subsidies, would permit the trust to distribute grants to other than central government departments to assist in the protection of "open space" and to undertake a general educational programme to widen public appreciation of the need to protect the New Zealand landscape.

Long Wait For No Reward

Eighty-two-year-old Miss R. M. Belton braved the rain and the long wait to see the royal yacht Britannia berth at Princes Wharf at midday yesterday but glimpsed not so much as a royal wave.

Wearing her Queen Alexandra's Imperial Military Nursing Service medal for the occasion, Miss Belton caught a taxi from an Auckland rest home to see the Queen "for the last time."

It was not until the yacht had berthed that many people waiting at the wharf realised that the Queen was not on board but had gone from Devonport by car.

Royal Baby Souvenir

DAILY EXPRESS

THE VOICE OF BRITAIN

No. 24,070   Wednesday November 16 1977   8p   ★★★

In the face of the Queen last night–the joy of a granny visiting her first grandchild

BOY OH BOY!

Express Staff Reporters

DON COOLICAN, GABRIELLE FAGAN, PHILIP BELSHAM, ASHLEY WALTON, PATRICK CLANCY, JOHN KING

A PROUD Princess Anne showed off her baby to the Queen last night and told nurses: "He's marvellous."

Anne cuddled the 7lb 9oz boy and excitedly greeted her mother after sleeping off the exhaustion of the trouble-free birth.

The Queen, clearly delighted in her new role as grandmother, stayed for half an hour chatting in Anne's hospital room.

Beaming father Captain Mark Phillips, who held his wife's hand when he watched the birth yesterday morning, completed the happy family group. His first reaction to his son: "A great little chap."

As they talked, they all kept taking a peek at the tiny sleeping bundle in the cot beside Anne's bed.

And they discussed possible Christian names for the untitled Master Phillips, who has blue eyes and dark hair. No final decision has been made.

The Queen, who triumphantly broke the news at a startled Palace investiture hours earlier, waved to onlookers as she left St Mary's Hospital, Paddington.

They cheered and shouted their

Page 2, Column 3

PICTURE BY REG LANCASTER

After half-an-hour's chat and several peeks at her sleeping grandson
... the delighted Queen leaving St. Mary's hospital last night

To Anne and Mark, a son: Pages 2, 3, 19 and Centre Pages

WEATHER : Showers, strong winds—Details Page 2 ● TV and Radio Pages 22. 23 ● Finance Pages 30, 31 ● Sport starts Page 33 ● Target, Crosswords and your favourite strips Page 32

JUBILEE Mirror

Daily Mirror Souvenir Special — June 3, 1977

HAPPY ANNIVERSARY!

HAPPY and glorious: the smiling Queen.

—from the Mirror and 12-million readers

THERE will be a smile on the face of Britain next week . . . a smile that says Happy Anniversary to the best-loved lady in the land . . . a smile that mirrors the affection the whole world feels for our Queen.

She has one of the world's most demanding jobs. It takes endless diplomacy, unlimited charm and almost superhuman stamina.

Her anniversary is going to be the biggest British beano for decades. That's why we echo the National Anthem's hope that she will be: LONG TO REIGN OVER US.

MAGIC SMILES: From the thousands of Royal pictures taken by Mirror photographers comes this favourite, dated Sierra Leone 1961, for our Jubilee salute

MAGIC MOMENT: The formalities are forgotten as the state visit to Germany in 1965 provides this moment to treasure for two little girls.

Daily  Mail

WEDNESDAY, JUNE 8, 1977

8p (CHANNEL ISLANDS 9p)

The Queen says it for all of us

IS EVERYBODY HAPPY? I AM!

THIS was the moment that really captured the spirit of the Jubilee as the Queen walked among the people packed together outside St Paul's Cathedral. The happiness that until then had been almost visibly kept in check bubbled from her. 'Everybody quite happy?' she asked one set of cheering spectators who had suffered the indifferent weather for hours. Then before they could answer she replied for herself. And there was no doubting it : 'I am.' Then later : 'What a lovely day, we are so lucky.' The Queen's walk from the cathedral to Guildhall was scheduled to last 20 minutes. In fact it took almost twice as long. But time didn't matter—by now it really was the day for the Queen and the people. The laughing faces around her tell the story.

 INSIDE your special Jubilee Mail: Royal Walkabout 2, 3, Shaun Usher's view 6, Barbara Griggs on the Fashions 13, Photo Extra 23-26

BRITAIN'S BIGGEST EVENING SALE

Evening News

NIGHT SPECIAL CLOSING PRICES

LONDON: WEDNESDAY MAY 10 1978 8p

Kensington Palace announce the end of a royal marriage

MARGARET: A DIVORCE

PRINCESS MARGARET and Lord Snowdon are to seek a divorce. The news came in an announcement from Kensington Palace this afternoon.

It said: "Her Royal Highness The Princess Margaret, Countess of Snowdon, and the Earl of Snowdon, after two years of separation have agreed that their marriage should formally be ended. Accordingly Her Royal Highness will start the necessary legal proceedings."

The Princess is confined to bed in hospital, suffering from suspected gastro enteritis. Lord Snowdon, according to his secretary, was this afternoon "on a photo assignment in London, working hard as he normally does."

Married 18 years

A Kensington Palace spokesman said the Princess had "no plans for re-marriage."

He added: "Of course, we are not in a position to comment about Lord Snowdon."

Proceedings were already under way and the 47-year-old Princess will be represented by the Queen's solicitor, Mr. Matthew Farrer.

He said: "The Princess is suing for divorce. This is a technicality, one party has to start the proceedings.

"The marriage has broken down and the couple have lived apart for two years. These are obviously the grounds for divorce."

The spokesman said that the Princess was "making progress" in hospital and he added: "The result of tests taken by the doctors will not be known until Friday."

The Queen, who is at Buckingham Palace this afternoon, has been kept informed. But no constitutional consent is needed in matters of this sort, said the spokesman.

Custody of children

The couple, who separated in March, 1976, after 18 years of marriage, ave two children, Viscount Linley, aged 16, and Lady Sarah Armstrong-Jones 13, and the Princess will continue to have custody of them.

The Kensington Palace spokesman made it clear that the couple will continue to be friends. "Naturally Princess and Lord Snowdon

Before the break . . Princess Margaret and Lord Snowdon with Lord Linley and Lady Sarah Armstrong-Jones.

will continue to see each other on the same friendly basis as they have with each other over the last two years."

Since the separation Lord Snowden has become a close friend of Lucy Lindsay-Hogg, daughter of the clothing manufacturer Donald Davies. She was not at her Kensington home this afternoon.

Roddy Llewellyn, Princess Margaret's friend is on holiday in Marrakesh, Morrocco.

Divorce will not alter the Princess's position. She will keep her title and her position in Royal circles, and, said the spokesman: "She will continue

her Royal duties as soon as she is fit enough. It is purely coincidental that Princess Margaret is in hospital. These arrangements were well under way before she became ill and her illness has nothing to do with the pending proceedings."

Financial arrangements between the Princess and her husband will also continue to be the same, but these are not being made public.

Solicitors of both the Princess and Lord Snowdon have been in close touch for some time and "Formal proceedings will begin within days."

TV: 24

ENTERTAINMENT: 14

DAILY Mirror

PHOTO FINISH!

Thursday, June 8, 1978

WHAT A THRILLER ! The Queen and Lord Porchester, her racing manager, watch the nail-biting Derby finish.   Picture: MIKE MALONEY.

Fans pelt the Scots

From ALASDAIR BUCHAN in Cordoba

FURIOUS Scottish fans threw stones and tried to break into their team's coach as it left the scene of a dismal World Cup effort last night.

Ally MacLeod's "Tartan Army" had just managed to scrape a 1—1 draw with no-hopers Iran.

Only an own-goal by an Iranian defender saved the Scots from defeat.

The worst abuse was reserved for manager Ally when he left the dressing room at the Cordoba stadium last of all.

One angry fan shouted : "We walked a million miles for you!"

And another group of fans chanted : "It's all for the money ! "

Supporters making the V-sign chanted : "Ally out—Ally out ! "

A wailing police car and heavy police guard failed to keep the angry Scottish fans at bay.

Earlier, a dozen were taken into police custody after police spotted an obscene banner in a nearby cafe.

Following Holland's 0-0 draw with Peru last night, Scotland must now beat Holland by three clear goals to get into the next round.

After last night's results, bookies were quoting Scotland at a staggering 5,000-1 to win the Cup.

● World Cup Special — Page 31 and Back Page.

Derby picture to remember

IT'S the greatest Royal picture of the year.

It was taken by Mirror cameraman Mike Maloney at the finish of the greatest race of the year, the Epsom Derby.

And it uniquely captured the Queen's bubbling excitement as her favourite sport of horse-racing turned on a majestic show.

The Queen's own runner, English Harbour, which trailed in eighteenth of the 25 starters, might have given her little to cheer about. But she was on her feet with everyone else as Shirley Heights beat Hawaiian Sound in a dramatic photo finish.

Just the length of a horse's head robbed 46-year-old American Willie Shoemaker, on Hawaiian Sound of a fairytale success in his first Epsom Derby ride. But like the Queen, Willie shrugged off the disappointment of losing. "A brilliant ride," said one consoling chap. "Nearly brilliant," replied Willie.

● Portrait of a royal punter—Page 3
● Racing Mirror—Pages 28 and 29

MURDER OF LORD LOUIS

Mountbatten and 15 soldiers killed by IRA

Earl Mountbatten, victim of Ireland's Murderous Monday

Daily Mail Reporters

IN a day of unparalleled horror in Ireland, Lord Mountbatten of Burma, the Queen's cousin, and 15 British paratroopers were murdered by the IRA.

The killings were cowardly and callous.

Lord Mountbatten died when a bomb planted on his converted fishing boat exploded half a mile off Co. Sligo on the West coast of the Irish Republic.

His 15-year-old grandson, the Hon Nicholas Brabourne, also died in the blast and so did his boatman, Paul Maxwell, also 15.

Lord Mountbatten's daughter, Lady Patricia Brabourne, 55, her husband Lord Brabourne, 54, the Dowager Lady Brabourne, 82, and Nicholas's twin brother, Timothy, also were on board and were taken to hospital.

Last night the two women and Timothy were seriously ill in a hospital intensive care unit. Timothy was believed to be in danger of losing an eye. Lord Brabourne was said to be badly hurt and in a general surgical ward.

The Provisional IRA said similar radio-controlled bombs were used to

Turn to Page Two Col. 1

End of a legend: Mountbatten's body is taken from the boat which brought it to shore

Picture album of a royal life—a four-page tribute to ' Uncle Dickie ' starts in Page 15.

Melbourne's Queen

The Herald 15c

63-0211 63-0351 CLASSIFIED MELBOURNE, WEDNESDAY, MAY 28, 1980 38 PAGES

THE QUEEN first met Melbourne's number one citizen the Lord Mayor, Cr Bernardi, outside the Town Hall, then walked across Swanston St. to meet the people.

The Flower Lady . . .

Melbourne greeted the Queen today — with flowers.

Spectators crammed Swanston St. 10 deep to welcome the Queen as she strolled to the City Square.

It was children's day. Dozens of young children streamed across the street to thrust flowers into her hands.

The Queen stopped many times during her walk with the Premier, Mr Hamer, to talk to people.

She could not walk more than a few paces without flowers, ranging from garden - picked posies - to florists' bouquets, being thrust into her hands.

In all her walks — and they started in Melbourne 10 years ago — the Queen has never received so many blooms.

As her arms filled, she kept handing them to her Lady-in-waiting, Lady Susan Hussey.

Lady Susan in the end had to pass them to other royal tour officials.

Davis Austin, 3, of North Fitzroy, was ushered across the road to say hello to the Queen.

She thanked Narelle Forbes, 9, of Cowper St., Essendon North, for a bunch of violets.

"They smell beautiful," the Queen said to Narelle.

"Thank you very much."

Edward Dugdale, a Monash University engineering student, whose mother, Mrs Katherine Dugdale, is one of the Queen's ladies in waiting, was spotted in the crowd and taken to meet the Queen.

The Queen also stopped

briefly to chat with Mrs Margaret McCullagh, of Ascot Vale, who is 131 years old.

"She's just lovely," said Mrs McCullagh, who was waiting at the square in a wheelchair, with a copy of the telegram the Queen sent her last year when she turned 100.

Thousands of Union Jacks and Australian flags fluttered as the Queen, then the Duke, stepped from the open car at the corner of Swanston and Bourke Sts.

More pictures — Page 3

CONTINUED ON PAGE 3

ROAD TOLL
This year 268
Last year 326

It was flowers all the way for the Queen when she walked down Swanston St. The Premier, Mr Hamer looks on as the Queen gathers another armful.

No. 31,518. — Registered for posting as a publication Category B and registered as a newspaper at the British Post Office.

FORECAST: City. — Rain in East. Few showers west, cool E. to S.E. wind. — Page 13.

Daily Mail

WEDNESDAY, JULY 16, 1980   12p

Royal souvenir edition

Queen Mother shows 'the human face of royalty'

THAT SMILE!

And a royal wave to the joyful crowd

By BRIAN JAMES

SHE turned on the steps of St Paul's and in the wind the loose chiffon shoulders of her lilac dress flew free like a cape . . . the Wonder Woman of the Royal set.

Queen Elizabeth the Queen Mother yesterday put on a smile undamaged by a million outings and listened to London's greeting for her 80th birthday.

Then she turned and went inside the cathedral, there to hear Archbishop Runcie get it right, absolutely right, when he declared she has shown 'the human face of royalty'.

That was why, as the sun filled the skies, the capital had filled its streets to wave at and wonder at the endless warmth of this, the ultimate Grannie.

It was a day of pomp, naturally, on the famous route from Buckingham Palace to St Paul's, two miles along which the courts and corteges have rumbled for centuries,

Turn to Page 2 Col. 1

For the mother A loving smile from the Queen during yesterday's service at St Paul's Cathedral

For the crowd A classic wave from the day's heroine as she stands on the steps of St Paul's to salute those who have lined the route to cheer her

INSIDE: Femail 12, Diary 15, Prize Crossword 25, TV 26-27, Letters, Stars & Strips 30, Motor, Cycling 31, Classified 31-35, Sport 35-40

THE Sun

Saturday, October 18, 1980   12p   TODAY'S SPORT STARTS ON PAGE 25

BLACK MAGIC

Velvet Queen wows them at the Vatican!

Reigning in Rome . . . the Queen in velvet splendour with the Pope at the Vatican

From JAMES LEWTHWAITE In Rome

THE QUEEN wore black to go to the Vatican yesterday . . . and the effect was magical.

She looked magnificent for her private audience with Pope John-Paul II.

Even fashion-conscious Rome was wowed by her beautiful full-length velvet-and-taffeta gown.

Because of Papal protocol the Queen had to wear black — a colour many women try to avoid. But she turned it into a royal triumph.

Fashion experts who have seen her on numerous tours could not remember when she looked so regal.

Her black cascade veil was held in place by a superb diamond tiara. Her gown sparkled with more jewels, including the diamond of the Garter on her sleeves.

Around her neck were double-choke pearls, and a tiny diamond glistened on her wrist.

CHEERED

As she swept along the normally quiet corridors of the Vatican, young trainee priests cheered their heads off

It was a great triumph for the Queen's youngest and latest dress designer, Ian Thomas.

Royal favourite Hardy Amies had designed a dress in black lace, but the Queen preferred Thomas's creation.

The audience—the first State visit to the Vatican by a British monarch—was also a great success

The Queen and Prince Philip talked with Pope John Paul for 42 minutes, 17 minutes longer than scheduled.

They spoke in English, one of the Pope's favourite languages, and afterwards they swapped gifts.

The Pope presented the Queen with a set of leather-bound volumes of The Divine Comedy.

Continued on Page Two

NEXT WEEK IS EXTRA-SPECIAL IN YOUR EXCITING SUN

WHAT DO YOU WEAR IN BED?

5 FORD FESTIVALS TO BE WON

IDIOTS' COOK BOOK By RICHARD O'SULLIVAN

WHAT TEENAGERS REALLY THINK See Centre Pages

105

Sunday Mirror

22p   June 14, 1981   No. 943

Six pistol cracks ring out—then the sudden fear.. 'Has the Queen been shot?'

THE AWFUL MOMENT

■ THIS was the awful moment in London yesterday when six shots rang out as the Queen rode past.

■ A MOUNTED police officer still has his hand raised to salute Her Majesty on her way to the Trooping the Colour ceremony.

■ SIX pistol cracks sounded and the sudden fear was: "Has the Queen been shot?"

■ BUT even before the echoes of the shots died away a policeman, shirt-tail showing, is pictured dashing to grab a youth.

■ THE PC was halfway across The Mall before many in the crowd had time to turn their heads to see where the shots came from.

■ POLICE, an ambulanceman, and even members of the public pounced on the gunman — who fired a starting pistol using blanks.

■ LATER a 17-year-old youth was charged under the Treason Act.

The Queen reins back to control her frightened horse as a policeman runs towards the gunman.   Picture: DAVID KILBURN

TREASON CHARGE
—Back Page

Full story
—Centre Pages

THE Sun

WAGNER TO WED AGAIN

Robert Wagner... in love again

See Centre Pages

Jill St John. his next bride

QUEEN SPOKE TO PROWLER AT HER BEDSIDE

The Queen ... cool courage with intruder

Prince Philip ... he was in another bedroom

Ten-minute chat..then she escaped from room

THE QUEEN had an amazing face-to-face meeting with a prowler in her bedroom, it was revealed last night.

The intruder sat on her bed and chatted to her for 10 minutes before a footman came to her rescue.

The drama began after the prowler got into the Queen's bedchamber at Buckingham Palace—an unprecedented breach of security.

As he sat on the Queen's bed, she woke up ... and calmly started to talk to him.

Then he asked for a

By HARRY ARNOLD and SHAN LANCASTER

cigarette and the Queen saw her chance to escape. She stepped into the corridor and alerted her footman.

The footman walked quickly into the bedchamber and calmly overpowered the intruder.

But a North Country chambermaid who saw him being taken away let slip a horrified remark.

The Queen, greatly amused, later mimicked her terrified squeak of: "Bloody hell, ma'am, what's he doing in

there?" Last night, a senior detective paid tribute to Her Majesty's quick thinking and courage.

"The Queen was very brave. By being calm she did not alarm the man," he said.

"He might have panicked and it could

have been a very different story.

"It is the most incredible story of how someone can walk in off the street and end up in the Queen's bedroom."

At the time of the incident last Friday, Prince Philip was sleeping in a

Continued on Page Four

EXCLUSIVE: Security scare at Di's home—See Page 4

DAILY Mirror

Fury over Royal security

Tuesday, July 13, 1982   16p   *

HOW could a man break into the Palace . . . TWICE?

WHY did police take thirty minutes to arrive?

The questions facing Home Secretary Whitelaw and Yard chief McNee

SEE PAGES TWO, THREE, THIRTEEN, FOURTEEN and FIFTEEN

DAILY EXPRESS

Tuesday July 20 1982 ● 17p ● Weather : Sunny spells **THE VOICE OF BRITAIN**

SCANDAL
of the man who guarded the Queen

By JOHN WARDEN, ALAN COCHRANE and ANDREW TAYLOR

T H E SCANDAL over the Queen's protection grew last night when it was revealed that her personal bodyguard, Scotland Y a r d Commander Michael Trestrail, resigned after admitting a homosexual relationship with a m a l e prostitute.

A grim Home Secretary Mr William Whitelaw gave the news to the Commons.

It means that for years the Queen's safety depended on a policeman who was open to blackmail.

Mr Whitelaw was faced with this new security outrage immediately following the case of the intruder in the Queen's bedroom.

Yesterday Michael Fagan was sent for trial at the Old Bailey—for stealing wine from the Palace in June. He will not face charges over the bedroom incident.

The Fagan and Trestrail cases are not directly connected—last night Mr Whitelaw firmly denied that Fagan was the man involved with the commander—but the repercussions from both are only beginning.

'Pillowtalk'

Mrs Thatcher's Government is now up against the most serious security scandal since the John Profumo-Christine Keeler affair nearly 20 years ago.

Once again the secrets of Throne or State have been potentially at the disposal of a prostitute to spread by way of "pillowtalk."

The risks to the Queen are beyond comprehension. For Commander Trestrail, a 51-year-old bachelor, was responsible for the Queen's safety whenever she was in public.

She was thus at possible risk to an assailant who needed warning of her public appearances, many details of which were security-classified.

As well as being a personal bodyguard Commander Trestrail was in charge of a Scotland Yard section code-named A1 responsible for security for all the Royal Family.

And despite the admission that he had had a homosexual relationship with the prostitute over a number of years, the commander's activities

The man at the Queen's elbow: Commander Trestrail on duty

failed to show up in any of the "postitive vetting" procedures he went through.

This is supposed to give security clearance of the highest order—delving deeply into personal background.

The degree of risk to the Queen is all the more apparent s i n c e the male prostitute has displayed no loyalty to Commander Trestrail.

Their relationship came to light only when the prostitute offered to sell his "confession" to the Sun newspaper following the row over Buckingham Palace security.

This alerted Palace officials, who informed Scotland Yard. Commander Trestrail, when confronted with the allegations by senior colleagues and MI5 men, resigned on Saturday.

But amazingly Mr Whitelaw did

not know until he arrived at his office at 9.15 am yesterday.

Within an hour he was in Downing Street telling Mrs Thatcher — who last night had a special audience of the Queen lasting 45 minutes.

MPs were asking why Prime Minister and Home Secretary were kept in the dark over the weekend and there were suspicions of another attempt to cover up the facts.

The scandal is s t i l l washing perilously close to the Home Secretary and the Metropolitan Police Commissioner Sir David McNee for a failure of administrative responsibility.

The exposure was a coincidence. It did not emerge from inquiries into the Palace break-in being made by Assistant Commissioner John Dellow.

If the male prostitute had not "confessed," the scandal might have gone undetected.

And it was widely believed that the commander's relationship with the prostitute lasted longer than the 10 years he had been guarding the Queen.

Statement

Mr Whitelaw's brief statement shocked the Commons into silence.

"Commander Trestrail, the Queen's Police Officer, has confessed to having a homosexual relationship over a number of years with a male prostitute." he said. "He has resigned from the Metropolitan Police."

It was Labour Independent Mr George Cunningham who asked the key question : "Are we to assume this information was not known to the security services until now ? Does that mean that no positive vetting was carried out or that there was positive vetting which failed to reveal the facts ?"

Mr Whitelaw could only reply : "He was positively vetted."

Last night, as anger mounted among MPs a white-faced Mr Whitelaw begged his critics to get off his back.

"Goodness knows, I have been lambasted enough by enough people," he said, as he went into a meeting of Tory backbenchers. "I am going to make a statement to the House on Wednesday, and that should be enough."

On the question of why he was not told about Commander Trestrail until yesterday morning he said : "There was no need for me to be told any earlier. It was perfectly proper. . . . Investigations were going on at the Palace."

After his meeting Mr Whitelaw insisted he had no intention of

Page 2, Column 5

 The quiet man who was never far away

PAGES 2 & 3

 Scandal that grows and grows—Peter McKay

PAGE 6

 Tortured mind of Michael Fagan

CENTRE PAGES

DAILY Mirror HOME

Saturday, September 18, 1982   16p   *

DATELINE: Portsmouth

'There were times when I was really terrified. But I would say to myself, I'm going to survive come hell or high water'

See Pages 2, 3 and 7

HIS ROYAL HAPPINESS: Jubilant Prince Andrew, ashore with proud Prince Philip after the carrier Invincible sailed home from the Falklands to a tumultuous welcome at Portsmouth yesterday.   **Picture: KENT GAVIN**

BINGO £1,000,000

Play it once, play it twice
See Page 12

The Times
OF SWAZILAND

Price 15 cents   Tuesday, October 26, 1982   Vol. 80 No. 194

WHIRLWIND TOUR A REAL 'SMILING SAFARI'

PRINCESS MEETS HER 'CHILDREN'

A RADIANT Princess Anne yesterday met the children of Swaziland ... and they loved her.

The Princess's whirlwind three-day visit to the kingdom was a real "smiling safari" as she visited three separate children's projects in the Hhohho District.

Wherever she stopped on her tour, Princess Anne was surrounded by happy, smiling children and she responded to their warm welcome by spending long periods chatting to them.

By JAMES DLAMINI

In fact the Princess was so at home chatting to the kids that at times her tight schedule was threatened and officials with her were left anxiously checking their watches.

The Princess, who is president of the Save the Children Fund, arrived in Swaziland on Sunday to visit the Fund's projects here.

Princess Anne drove by car from the Royal Guest lodge just outside Lobamba to Ntfonjeni, deep inside the bundu.

The tour party was temporarily joined by Prince Gabheni at Ntfonjeni. She was greeted by a long line of children who had been anxiously waiting for her arrival.

They cheered and stampeded into a hall where the function was to be conducted. In the hall, the children met her with a hymn.

After hymns, schools choirs performances were conducted. Two children then provided her with gifts and flowers.

There is a Save the Children Fund feeding project at Ntfonjeni school. "We feel we're the luckiest school in Swaziland," said an official when the Princess departed amid more cheers from the children.

From Ntfonjeni she proceeded to Emkhuzweni Rural health centre. From Ntfonjeni to Emkhuzweni, it is a long dusty drive through scrubland. The centre is run by the Holiness

PICTURES ON PAGES 6 AND 7

Union Mission which has some immunisation equipment purchased by Save the Children Fund.

"Its like a mini hospital. We do all sorts of things, including operations here," one of the staff members was heard telling the Princess during the tour of the centre.

In the centre, she visited the outpatients department where she occasionally stopped and chatted with patients. She also visited the wards, where she would also stop and chat with patients lightheartedly for some time.

The management of the clinic provided her with a light lunch before she proceeded to the Nkamanzi Rural Immunisation Centre.

The Nkamanzi is a joint Swaziland government and Save the Children Fund project.

She watched as a children's mass immunisation was being conducted under a tree for lack of accomodation. The
(Back Page Col.3)

Her Royal Highness, Princess Anne chatting to Prince Gabheni, Minister for Home Affairs at Ntfonjeni yesterday.

MOURNING: 57 FINED

A TOTAL of 57 people have been fined for refusing to honour the mourning directive.

Twenty-nine of them were fined a total of E1,740 by the Nhlangano National Court last week.

Others have been fined by the Manzini and Bhunya National Courts.

Almost all the accused told the courts they could not cut their hair because it

By MASHUMI TWALA

was against their religious beliefs.

At the Nhlangano National Court, the court president called for order when seven accused, calling themselves Jehova's Witnesses, started preaching to the court.

They opened their bibles and quoted several verses to support their defence.

Chief Jeremiah Dlamini of the Vusweni area, where the seven "Witnesses" stay, told the court that when the Royal Directive for mourning was issued, he summoned all his subjects and notified them.

He said: "These seven pointed out blankly that they could not afford to do that as it is against their religion. I warned them that they could be prosecuted if they refused."

"A few days later, I was notified that these people were determined not to cut their hair because, it would not be proper for them. That is when I decided to take action and brought them to the police."

In their defence, the Witnesses said: "We heard the
(Back Page Col.6)

CHAPTER 6

PRINCE CHARLES

Charles was born and raised beneath an unremitting spotlight of personal publicity.

Prince Charles has been a focus of attention to the world's press since the moment it was announced in 1948 that his mother was pregnant. He was born and raised beneath an unremitting spotlight of personal publicity for which he has not always been grateful. But in his adulthood — with occasional exceptions — it has been his natural good humour with journalists and photographers which has helped maintain his high public popularity.

Charles's parents took the unprecedented step of sending their son to school with other children, rather than having him privately educated behind the Palace walls. There were bound to be problems — and they began even during his first few days at a fashionable London day school, where normal daily life ground to a halt as a throng of journalists blocked the front entrance.

During his first term at Cheam prep school, the place was so beseiged by reporters and photographers that the entire educational experiment was in danger of being called off. The Queen's press secretary summoned all national newspaper editors to Buckingham Palace and warned them: leave the Prince in peace, or his public education will have to be abandoned — and it will all be the fault of the British press. The chastened editors complied.

But when Charles arrived at Gordonstoun, it all started again. Some of his exercise books were stolen from his desk and published in a German magazine. Then one day while out on a school expedition, he was spotted by a freelance journalist — forever after known to him as *that* woman — as he ordered a cherry brandy in a hotel bar. The heir to the throne did not know of a law against buying drinks in bars when only 14. "The whole world," as he put it, "exploded around my ears."

The press scarcely needed such highlights to give them an excuse for front pages about Charles. But he continued to provide them. Just before his investiture as Prince of Wales at Caernarvon in 1969 (p.119), the greatest Royal occasion since the Queen's coronation, he took part in a Cambridge University revue which had the newspapers beside themselves with delight (p.118). When he went on to win a university degree, the first member of the Royal Family ever to do so, newspapers of course cast doubt — quite unfairly — on its authenticity.

His ensuing years in the Services marked the beginning of the press's ten-year quest to find Prince Charles a bride. They had published their first helpful lists of eligible European princesses as long ago as his mother's accession to the throne, when the suitor was just three years old. But now the Prince was out of his teens, every girl spotted on his arm was billed Britain's next Queen. Acres of forest were felled to feed the flow of newsprint about Charles's marital intentions. In 1977 the *Daily Express* even managed to marry him off "officially" to the Roman Catholic Princess Marie-Astrid of Luxembourg. "The formal engagement," it declared confidently, "will be announced from Buckingham Palace on Monday."

It wasn't. And there was one face conspicuous by its absence from the constant picture panoramas of potential brides-to-be — a shy young English Rose 13 years Charles's junior named Lady Diana Spencer. Not until a zoom lens caught them cuddling by a trout stream in Scotland did Fleet Street catch up with the truth.

And then it didn't let go. Diana's ensuing ordeal by press was her first real lesson in the problems of becoming Royal. She passed it with flying colours, laying false trails, dodging the most remorseless of the "Royal-watchers" with unfailing charm and grace.

Their wedding in 1981 was the biggest media event of all time, launching almost as many books as special newspaper supplements. The fairy story continued within a year with the birth of a male heir, in direct line of succession, Prince William. Only once during three years of pursuit by press has Diana flagged — while pregnant, when the paparazzi got just too much for her. Among genuine fears that she might suffer a miscarriage, the editors were again summoned and told to call off their dogs.

Since that unhappy episode, the Princess of Wales has become such a worldwide media superstar that her husband has occasionally had to be content with a back seat. She was the undoubted star of their triumphant tours of Australia and Canada in 1983 (pp.125-127). Diana's mother-in-law could rest asssured that a new generation of Royalty could not have been more successfully launched.

If you look at the passing Royal pageant as a soap opera, as most British newspapers do, the arrival of the photogenic "Shy Di" amid the cast of characters could not have been bettered by Hollywood. Her charm and beauty are enough to ensure that her husband and son will enjoy a glorious progress towards the throne.

DAILY GRAPHIC

and DAILY SKETCH

Thursday, December 16, 1948 ★★★ A Kemsley Newspaper 1d.

THE PRINCE CHRISTENED

First picture of the Royal baby

Prince Charles of Edinburgh, a month and a day old, in the arms of his mother after his christening at Buckingham Palace yesterday. More pictures on Middle and Back Pages

SUNDAY GRAPHIC

No. 1,805 November 13, 1949 ℝ A Kemsley Newspaper 2d.

1 YEAR OLD

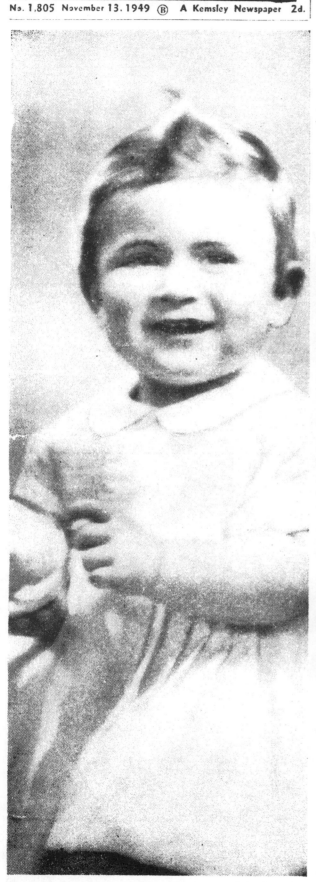

Nearly a year old, Prince Charles—a big boy for his age—reveals his new teeth (he now has six) in a delightful smile.

Jean Simmons and top Rank stars in exclusive preview of Royal Command Film fashions—See P.8

"Just a family party" for Prince's birthday

PRINCE CHARLES will be one to-morrow. But though all Britain will be wishing the baby Prince "happy birthday," there will be no official celebrations. By Princess Elizabeth's own wish, there will be just a small family party, to be held either at the Princess's country home at Windlesham Moor, or at Clarence House, where the little Prince's simply-furnished, white-walled day nursery looks out over The Mall.

The Duke of Edinburgh (to whom Princess Elizabeth was able a few days ago to send the message: "Charles has taken his first few steps alone") is, of course, serving with the Mediterranean Fleet and will not be there to enjoy the little party.

He has had his present flown over from Malta, where he is stationed, for Princess Elizabeth to give to the baby Prince.

These delightful studies of Princess Elizabeth and Prince Charles were specially taken for the occasion by Marcus Adams.

Now turn to Page Six for more pictures and for the full story of Prince Charles' first year, by Betty Spencer Shew, Court Correspondent to Exchange Telegraph.

DAILY GRAPHIC
DAILY & SKETCH

Friday, November 14, 1952 ★★★★★ A Kemsley Newspaper 2d.

Prince Charles is 4 to-day

SOUVENIR PICTURE NUMBER

Prince Charles is four years old to-day. In this new picture, with Princess Anne, he holds the watch his mother played with when photographed at the same age. The Prince's toys: Pictures on Middle Pages and Page 10.

Daily Mirror

THURS APR. 15 1954

1½d FORWARD WITH THE PEOPLE

No. 15,681

BEVAN WALKS OUT

MR. ANEURIN BEVAN dropped a political bombshell last night. He resigned from Labour's Shadow Cabinet —the Parliamentary Committee that decides Party policy in the Commons.

He will now sit among the Labour back-benchers — instead of beside the Party leaders—in the House.

Mr. Bevan, in a statement, said he resigned because he disagreed with the Party's policy on German rearmament and Indo-China.

● *The drama of the walk-out is told on the Back Page.*

We're going to see Mummy

GOODBYE, CHARLES AND ANNE SPECIAL PICTURES

Prince Charles, with Princess Anne looking on, shakes hands with Rear-Admiral A. G. Hubback, Admiral Superintendent of Portsmouth Dockyard, before the children sailed to meet the Queen at Tobruk, North Africa. On the bridge of the Royal yacht Britannia Prince Charles asked the captain: "Please can I steer Mummy's ship?" *More pictures on Pages 6, 8, 9 and the Back Page.*

DAILY SKETCH

Thursday, June 20, 1963   Price Threepence   ★★★   WEATHER: Cool, but sunny

Just a wee deoch an' doris for Charles—then what a row

BEND OVER, YOUR ROYAL HIGHNESS!

CLEO

The **REAL** story as only **FERGUS CASHIN** can tell it
Today on P. 8

By EDWARD CONNOLLY

PRINCE CHARLES may be in for a caning when he gets back to Gordonstoun School on Sunday—all because he drank a cherry brandy in an hotel cocktail bar.

Mr. Robert Chew, 55-year-old headmaster of Gordonstoun—Prince Philip is an old boy—said last night he was considering taking "disciplinary action" against the Prince, but could not say what form it would take until he had seen him to obtain the full story.

The 14 - year - old Prince's sip of liqueur in the Crown Hotel, Stornaway, Scotland, last Monday evening was admitted yesterday by Buckingham Palace after an earlier denial of the incident.

A Palace statement said Mr. Chew and the Queen's Press Secretary had been misled by a telephone call from the detective-bodyguard who was with the Prince when he toured the town.

STILL SAILING

Prince Charles left the bar—where he was sitting with Old Gordonstounian Mr. Harris Mackenzie, after Det.-Cons. D. Green walked in and said: "What are you doing in here?"

Outside in the hotel lobby, Det. Green asked the Prince: "What did you have?"

Said Charles: "A cherry brandy. That is all I knew what to ask for."

Last night Prince Charles was still on a training cruise off the Scottish coast.

At the time of the incident he and three other Gordonstoun boys were being shown round Stornaway by 32-year-old Mr. Mackenzie, and were hav-
⟶ *Back Page*

Yard men talk to Astor and Profumo

By REGINALD FOSTER

MR. JOHN PROFUMO was interviewed for two hours by police yesterday.

Chief Inspector Sam Herbert and Detective-Sergeant John Burrows saw him in the offices of his solicitors, Theodore Goddard and Co., in the Temple.

The two officers also spent three hours interviewing Lord Astor at Cliveden earlier in the week.

Other well-known people are to be interviewed during the next few days.

CONFERENCE

The Scotland Yard officers are in charge of an investigation which has involved Dr. Stephen Ward. Their inquiries are not confined to the allegations against Ward, who is on remand accused of living wholly or partly on immoral earnings.

It was learned last night that Chief Inspector Herbert has been in conference with security officers.

The Commons is due to pass judgment on Mr. Profumo today.

The Government last night published a motion, agreed with the Opposition, condemning Mr. Profumo for "grave contempt" of the Commons.

ON GUARD

Police are keeping a 24-hour guard on Christine Keeler after anonymous telephone calls threatening her life.

Last night uniformed constables were patrolling the pavement outside the flat where she is living in Devonshire - terrace, Paddington, W.

The anonymous calls were made to three police stations and a newspaper office by a man who said he would kill Miss Keeler "within hours."

Prince Charles . . . faces "disciplinary action" when he returns to Gordonstoun on Sunday.

Sunday Mirror

7d.   March 2, 1969   No. 307

YIPPEE!

That's the new Royal word .. on the big day for Charles and Anne

SUDDENLY Princess Anne and Prince Charles emerged yesterday as Britain's liveliest youngsters. Charles, 20, set the pace. Giving his first radio interview he talked candidly of what it is really like to grow up as the future king. He quipped: "I didn't suddenly wake up in my pram one day and say 'Yippee!'" Turn to centre pages for his highly personalised account of the royal life— including his debut as a comic in Cambridge, recorded in the picture above. Anne, 18, also made a debut yesterday. In her first official engagement she took the salute and presented St. David's Day leeks to the Welsh Guards at Pirbright, Surrey. A proud day. Or to use a royal word—YIPPEE!

Daily Mirror YOUR PRINCE

5d. Wednesday, July 2, 1969 ◆ No. 20,377

MY MOST DEAR SON

THIS was the moving climax to a crowded day of breathtaking pageantry. The moment when the Queen presented the Prince of Wales to his people after his Investiture in Caernarvon Castle. She presented him as "my most dear son." That was the official description laid down in the Letters Patent, the historic form of words to be followed in creating any Prince of Wales. But no choice of words could have been more appropriate. For this was so clearly a mother proud of her son, raising his hand so gently.

With the world looking on, he had come through the pomp and the ceremony, the long ordeal, with compelling poise and dignity. And now, at last, he was ready to meet his people. As his mother raised his hand in the traditional manner of presentation, they smiled. At their people . . . and at each other.

MIRROR INVESTITURE SPECIAL on Pages 2, 3, 4, 5, 11, 15, 16, 17, 18, 19 and Back Page. Donald Zec's report starts on Page 15

THE Sun

WE SCOOP THE POOLS AGAIN!

Thursday, September 18, 1980   12p   TODAY'S TV: PAGES 14 and 15

IF IT'S NEWS IT'S IN THE No 1 SUN

Killer bug hits holiday Britons

● ONE Briton has died and five more are seriously ill in hospital with Legionnaires Disease.

● All six recently returned from holidays in the Rio Park Hotel at Benidorm, Spain, the source of previous outbreaks of the disease.

● Last night an alert went out to health authorities all over Britain.

Full story—Page 7

Dock strike peace deal

● DOCK leaders last night worked out a peace plan to avoid the crippling national strike threatened for Monday. Employment Secretary Jim Prior earlier offered extra cash to 178 dockers who faced the sack.

Full story—Page 2

West Ham fans on rampage

● WEST HAM soccer fans rioted as the London team went down 3-1 to Castilla in Spain last night. It was a bitter disappointment to the Second Division club, who had written to every supporter on the trip to Madrid asking for good behaviour.

Full story—Back Page

CHARLIE'S GIRL!

REVEALED . . Lady Diana poses with pupils Louise and Scarlett
Picture by ARTHUR EDWARDS

'You know I can't say anything about the Prince or my feelings for him'

THE bubbly blonde teenager tipped as the next Queen of England stepped regally into the limelight for the first time yesterday.

Prince Charles's new girl, vivacious 19-year-old Lady Diana Spencer, posed for photographers outside the kindergarten where she teaches.

But she refused to speak about her romance with the Prince. And that silence improved her chances of making the marriage f the century.

SERIOUS

For the youngest daughter of the Earl Spencer is the first serious girlfriend of the Prince who has kept mum.

As I strolled with her through the grounds of the Young England kindergarten, attached to St. Saviour's Church in London's Pimlico, Lady

By HARRY ARNOLD

Diana said: "You know I cannot say anything about the Prince or my feelings for him.

"I am saying that off my own bat. No one has told me to stay quiet."

But later she could not stay quiet when she was shown the pictures that were taken.

She was mildly embarrassed by the one which showed she was not wearing a slip under her cotton skirt, patterned with floral hearts.

"I was so nervous

Continued on Page Two

IN LOVE AGAIN!

Lady Di is the new girl for Charles

How The Sun broke the news on September 8

120

DAILY Mirror

Wednesday, February 25, 1981   12p

HIS ROYAL HIGHNESS
THE PRINCE OF
WALES PRESENTS:

MY
DI

**SOUVENIR
ISSUE**
**PLEASE TURN TO
BACK PAGE**
ALSO PAGES 2, 3, 7,
15, 16 AND 17

Printed by West of England Newspapers Ltd, Burrington Way, Plymouth, England.

DAILY
EXPRESS
Saturday July 25 1981 ● 15p ● Weather: Showers

THE VOICE OF BRITAIN

★★★

As Britain gets ready for the biggest party of all...

WE'RE OFF TO A WEDDING!

By JOHN McCORMICK

BRITAIN is preparing this weekend for a massive party to celebrate Wednesday's wedding of Prince Charles and Lady Diana.

London will be the centre, of course, with its pageantry, spectacle and crowds—but the joy will be reflected all over the land.

THE PAGEANTRY will be reinforced by visiting royals and Heads of State, revealed in the guest list announced by Buckingham Palace yesterday.

Consider the enormous security problems involved in looking after such a gathering at St Paul's, apart from our own Royal Family and leading figures of Church and State:—

America's Mrs Nancy Reagan, wife of the President.

Presidents of France, Greece, West Germany, Portugal and Iceland, and the Prime Minister of Turkey.

Ruling royals: Crown Prince and Princess of Japan, Princess Maha Chakri of Thailand, Crown Prince and Princess of Jordan, Prince and Princess of Nepal, Prince Hans Adam and Princess Mabie of Liechtenstein.

Ex-rulers: Michael and Anne of Rumania, Simeon and Margarita of Bulgaria, Constantine of Greece.

Commonwealth rulers: King and Queen of Tonga, Queen of Lesotho, Maliedoa Tanumafili of Western Samoa, Prince Gabieni and Princess Lindiow of Swaziland.

Presidents of Gambia, Malawi, Trinidad and Tobago, Sri Lanka, India, Cyprus, Naura, Kiribati, Dominica, Zimbabwe, Vanuata and Guyana, with wives representing those of Uganda, Ghana and Zambia.

Governors - General of Canada, Australia, New Zealand, Jamaica, Barbados, Mauritius, Fiji, Bahamas, Grenada, Papua New Guinea, Solomon Islands, and St Vincent and the Grenadines.

Vice-Presidents of Nigeria, Kenya and the Seychelles.

FIREWORKS

SPECTACLE: On Tuesday night, the eve of the wedding, Hyde Park will stage a huge fireworks display attended by the Queen, Prince Philip and Prince Charles.

The £65,000 cost is being met by worldwide TV rights, with the surplus going to charities for the disabled.

The show — based on one which took place in Green

Page 3 Column 3

TELEPHONE CHARGES TO GO UP BY 9½%

By PETER HITCHENS

TELEPHONE charges are to rise again in November by nine-and-a-half per cent.

The average cost of having a 'phone at home will increase by £20-a-year, while 5p in a 'phonebox will buy only two minutes of talking time.

The latest lift means 'phone charges have risen by more than a third since 1975—and British Telecom said last night that there could be more to come.

And they warned that home 'phone users face huge rental increases if the Government goes ahead with plans to bring free enterprise into the telephone business.

Telecom said: "The new tariff changes are the minimum consistent with our aims to continue to improve the telecommunications services of the nation and to meet the Government's financial targets."

Telegram charges are going up too—by 15 per cent.

Telecom's full year results due next month are expected to be down on last year's £236·1 million profit.

SKETCH BY BOB WILLIAMS

Come along and enjoy it with the

BRITAIN'S BEST TV AND RADIO GUIDE: SEE CENTRE PAGES

Weather Page 2 ● Express Woman Pages 10, 11 ● Gardening Page 19 ● Finance Pages 24, 25 ● Startime Page 26 ● Sport starts Page 27 ● Racing Pages 28, 29

DAILY STAR

A moment to treasure

ROYAL WEDDING

THURSDAY, JULY 30th, 1981   **12p** (13p C.I.s, 15p Eire) Printed in London

THE KISS

Daily Star picture by DAVID ASHDOWN

End of a perfect day—Back Page

On the Palace balcony for all the world to see, the tender kiss that sealed the nation's day of joy

WE'LL MEET AGAIN
Pages 22 and 23

The first official portrait of William – by Snowdon

DIANA AND HER BABY PRINCE

Daily Mail Reporter

INTRODUCING the most famous face of the 21st Century: Prince William of Wales, at 29 days old.

One day, as King, he will be on the coins, the stamps and the banknotes that our grandchildren and their children will use.

Already, he is the best-known baby in the world.

This first delightful official portrait of him with his mother the Princess of Wales is released today, his parents' first wedding anniversary.

It was taken nine days ago at Kensington Palace by William's great-uncle, Lord Snowdon, as was another on the centre pages. He said : 'I think the pictures speak for themselves if you want to know how the mother and baby are feeling. It was a great honour and a pleasure to be asked to take them.'

Prince Charles said when his son was born that William had the 'good fortune' not to look like him. The baby has blue eyes and fair hair like his mother, but then most babies have blue eyes at first and there does not seem to be enough hair yet to be significant.

So who does he take after? Is there, perhaps, a look of his royal grandmother ? Or even great-great-grandfather George V ? Within the family and now across the nation, the debate on such questions is, no doubt, only just beginning.

For the photo session, Prince William was in a long gown with lace edging and was posed on a cream lace cushion. Princess Diana, looking stunning, wore a cream silk dress with a necklace of cultured pearls set in diamonds with matching heart-shaped diamond earrings.

MOTHER, FATHER AND BABY PICTURE—CENTRE PAGES

LATE CITY

WEATHER: Brisbane, rain clearing.
Temperatures: Max. 28 degrees; Min. 22 degrees.
Tides: High 1.47 a.m. (2.2m), 1.57 p.m. (1.7m); Low 8.11 a.m. (0.7m), 8.05 p.m. (0.5m).
Full details on Page 12.

The Courier-Mail

OUR 136th YEAR
TODAY:
Motor-Mail

Phone 52 6011 Classified 52 0461 — **BRISBANE,** Monday, March, 21, 1983 — Recommended Price **25c** By Air Extra

Royal magic in Alice

John Hamilton
in Alice Springs

THERE could be no more beautiful time for a prince who loves Australia to bring a princess from the dreary, cold days of an English winter, 30 hours through time and space to land here in the dead heart of Australia.

For the Dead Heart has been transformed, as if by a sweep of a fairy godmother's wand, into a vibrantly alive, noisy, green oasis.

The two nights of heavy rain last week have worked their magic. By night the air resounds with the croak and bong of a hundred thousand bullfrogs rejoicing in the water of the creeks and rivers that are now coursing through the desert.

By day, huge flocks of galahs flash pink and grey as they screech and wheel over the white river gums, and the creeks' clean sands sparkle in the sun.

Grave groups of Aboriginals camp, cross-legged on the banks of the Todd River, and their children shrill and splash in the shallows.

The surrounding MacDonnell Ranges glow red and purple in sun and shadow and the mighty ancient heart of the continent throbs with life and the wonder of a broken drought.

But when the sun comes up in the Territory, the flies awake. And flies are no respecters of persons. One tiny black bush fly alighted on a chubby baby in a white romper suit with a red hatch pattern early yesterday morning.

His Royal Highness, Prince William, scuinted at the sun.

The Alice Springs bushfly did an exploratory sweep around his left eyelid.

"He's got the first fly on him," exalted the baby's father, Prince Charles. "We are going to bring him up the hard way."

Holding the baby, the Princess of Wales smiled a shy uncertain smile as the outback sun grew in strength and glowed golden on her soft English complexion.

Behind a token rope barrier, a scrambling horde of 49 photographers festooned with cameras and lenses set up a winding click of motor drive.

"This way Sir," "Sir, this way", "Sir, Sir . . ."

"Let's get organised," said Prince Charles, the old professional from the Palace. "Which way shall we look first?"

They looked this way, and then that.

"Say Dad-da," said an anxious little Cockney photographer shooting pictures with a noise like a hand crank machine gun.

"Not yet!" said Prince Charles laughing.

Princess Diana still smiled that uncertain smile and Prince William began showing signs that he was fed up.

In swept Nanny, in a blue frock and regulation white shoes, and before you could say Christopher Robin the baby was gathered up and was back aboard the RAAF Boeing 707 to be taken on in style to Albury and the sanctuary of Woomargama Station.

Mr Victor Chapman, the burly Canadian press secretary to Prince Charles, said he heard Prince William only twice during the journey. "I saw him four or five other times, and he travelled very well," he said.

Certainly the baby looked well, if slightly bemused by what was going on in front of the Alice Springs air terminal.

A man on a petrol tanker shouted "good on ya!" several times.

Another man with a heavy German accent shouted, "Vill the people in front sit down so we can see der Princess". Nobody sat down. Nobody sits down on Royal tours — it is a perpetual scramble.

Dozens of children pressed forward as Prince Charles and Princess Diana made their way to the terminal. Many of the kids had little posies of flowers, tied up with bits of string, or wrapped in sheaf of aluminium foil.

Princess Diana gave her white clasp bag to a lady-in-waiting, and began collecting flowers. Then the lady-in-waiting began collecting flowers too.

By the time the couple drove off in their white car, windows open, the kids were throwing their bouquets in at the Prince and Princess.

Perhaps 1500 people were at the terminal to watch the Royal arrival. When the crowd tried to leave the terminal, it caused the first big recorded traffic jam in Alice Springs' history.

Royal 'Bolt hole', Page 3

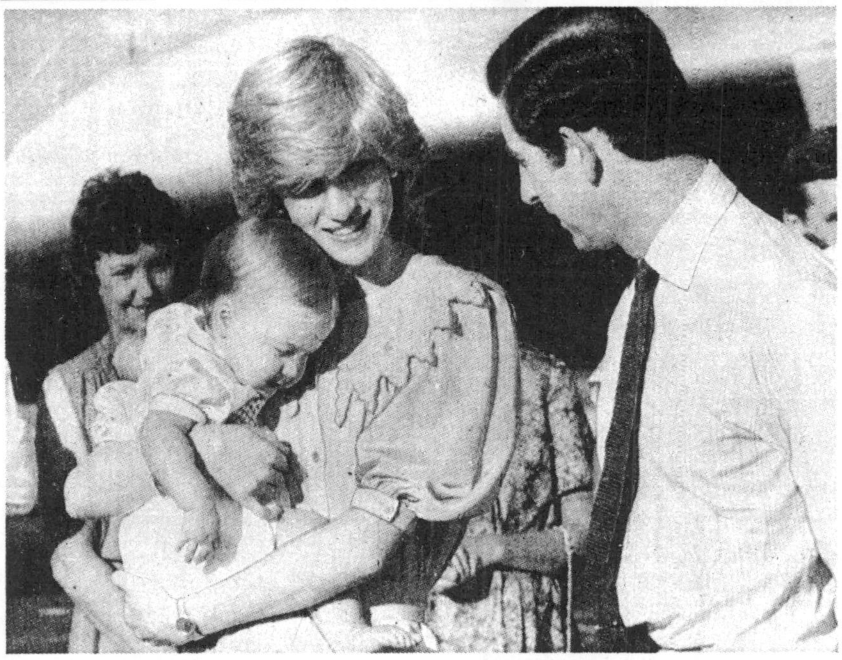

Prince Charles, Princess Diana and Prince William minutes after their arrival at Alice Springs.

Words not quoted

LAST evening I attended a cocktail party. It was in honor of two visiting people from England.

I'm not allowed to mention their names or what they had to say. Protocol forbids this.

But let us say there was a man — let's call him C for purposes of identification — in a brown safari suit.

And a slim young woman — let's call her D — in a white silk dress, splashed with red flowers on long green stems.

I chatted with C first. I gained the impression he had a love for Australia and it's people. I also gained the impression he thought its people said what they thought, which enabled him to say what he thought back.

Several thoughts were expressed. Ornithology was mentioned, and a bird called a Hawk.

Soon after the young lady — remember, we are calling her only for purposes of identification D — came into view.

Her feet seemed to be hurting because she shifted from one foot to the other. D is very tall and very thin. And very charming.

For some reason thoughts occurred about raising babies. D gave the impression she thinks she is very lucky because she has a placid baby who simply likes his bottle and sleeps well.

That is all I can say at this stage.

Except that it was a charming party with charming people, the drinks were cold, and the savories very pleasant, too.

Today

Entertainer

Actress Lorraine Bayly, formerly of The Sullivans and now in Carson's Law, discusses her work and the series, and former TV newsreader Brian Cahill talks about his move from the small screen to radio. Page 17.

MONDAY MONEY By Finance Editor JACK LUNN

A Brisbane stockbroker has participated in a United States equity issue. Jack Lunn has the details. Page 14

Motor-Mail

Motor Mail previews two new expensive "European thoroughbreds" just released on the Australian market — the BMW 520i and Alfa Romeo's GTV6. Page 15

Overseas

The Soviet Union has signalled a new move in the Middle East by announcing it has agreed to sign a friendship treaty with Libya, the United States' most bitter foe in the region. Page 6.

Sports-Mail

And in Brisbane rugby league, Wests caused a Woolies upset when it beat last year's grand finalists, Souths, 10-4. Barry Dick was at the game. Page 19.

ALSO INSIDE

World News...........6, 7
Churches..................10
Services.................. 12
Business.................. 14
Motor Mail................15
Living........................16
Entertainer.........17, 18
Sport..................19-22
Theatres...................22
Classified Index.......27

Good rain, but still a drought

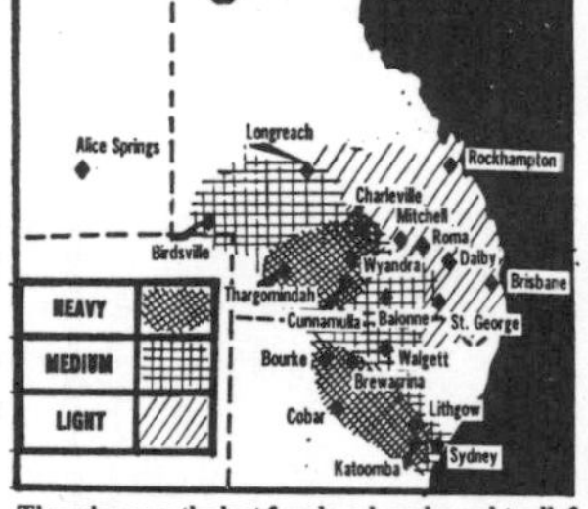

The rains over the last few days have brought relief to drought-stricken areas in central Queensland and northern New South Wales.

QUEENSLAND'S "Heartbreak Corner" had some of its wounds healed on the weekend when falls of up to 136 mm closed roads, isolated properties and delighted graziers.

By Rural Reporter, LISA McKEE

But according to the Weather Bureau, the rain should continue to move along the southern border of the State, and start clearing from Queensland today.

"There is still a lot of cloud around and there could be showers in some areas, but there will not be the general rain we have seen in the last few days," a spokesman said.

And in New South Wales, the rain that fell across the north-eastern half of the state could spell new life for drought-stricken livestock and grain growers.

A search is underway for three men missing in flood country near Eromanga (*story page 2*).

At Cunnamulla, the stranglehold of a five-year drought was eased when rain started falling at 4 a.m. on Saturday and continued to fall steadily until yesterday afternoon.

"The graziers think it is magic," Constable Ross Kruger of the Cunnamulla police said. "The only storms we get around here usually are dust storms."

The township of Thargomindah, where more than 125 mm fell in the 48 hours to 3 p.m. yesterday, is isolated by water which has crossed the road to Cunnamulla at Eulo in the east and flooded other exits from the town.

But the drought was far from broken, the Primary Industries Minister, Mr Ahern, said last night.

"There have been some useful falls, but it is by no means over. It is late in the season, the falls have been patchy, and follow-up rain will be needed."

Mr Ahern said he would recommend to cabinet today that a further four shires — Eidsvold, Mundubbera, Isis and Widgee — be added to the drought-declared list.

"If falls such as we have seen in the last few days are repeated a few times we might see an end to the worst drought in Australian history," he said.

The clouds had cleared at Birdsville yesterday, leaving the township still wallowing in 62 mm of rain which fell in the 24 hours to 9 a.m. Saturday. District Weather Bureau recorder, Mrs Dianne Goad, said the township was still cut off by the Diamantina River in the east, and water over the road to the south and north.

Continued Page 2

Wests win in wet

POURING rain in Brisbane yesterday did not stop the pre-season rugby league final between Wests and Souths at Lang Park. Souths second rower Ash Lumby attempts to break out of a tackle by Wests centre Len Standen. Wests won 10-4. Yesterday's rain did stop the second day's play in the four-day Brisbane club cricket final but the four football codes went ahead as scheduled. In Sydney, heavy rain caused the abandonment of the McDonald's Cup cricket final.

Full reports Pages 19, 20.

Man, two elephants killed in crash

A MAN and two elephants were killed last night when three semi-trailers in a caravan of circus trucks collided with each other 45 km south of Boggabilla, New South Wales, near the Queensland border.

Boggabilla police said the Sole Brothers Circus vehicles were travelling from Moree, NSW, to Goondiwindi on the Newell Highway when the accident occurred.

A semi-trailer travelling behind the group smashed into the rear of another semi-trailer which was pitched into the back of the leading vehicle.

Douglas Walter Buchal, 24, of Maribyrnong, Victoria, was driving the middle vehicle when he was killed.

He was a clown in the circus.

Police said two other men were injured and taken to Goondiwindi Hospital, where they were reported in satisfactory condition.

The elephants killed were in the trailer of the lead vehicle.

The circus, which was travelling from Moree in NSW, continued on to Goondiwindi. The owner of the circus, Mr Joe Perry, was distraught last night and today's scheduled performances are unlikely to go ahead.

Police were still attempting late last night to piece together the circumstances of the accident.

Birds under threat

From BRETT FREE

THE Gold Coast City Council will investigate plans to build a 15-storey building opposite the Currumbin bird sanctuary.

The call for the inquiry came from the Deputy Mayor, Ald. Sir John Egerton, who said the matter had caused enough public interest and concern to warrant an official council report.

Sir John's thoughts were endorsed by the other nine aldermen at last Friday's council meeting.

Residents fear a building permit issued two weeks ago will lead to a residential high-rise being built in the flight path of the thousands of lorikeets that feed at the sanctuary every day.

They claim birds would also be scared away by construction noises.

Dedicated park

The park assistant manger, Mr John Roe, said yesterday the birds were easily scared and "with the loud building noises, well you'd just about have to close the doors".

"The birds have been getting fewer and fewer in past years because of developments in the area. A lot of pople don't realise the park is here for all Australians.

"The park founder, Alex Griffiths, dedicated the park to the people of Australia when he handed it over to the National Trust in 1976."

The council health committee chairman, Ald. John Laws, said the council would have the right now allow the building to proceed.

"The land is zoned tourist facility, so council consent would have to be given before building could proceed," he said.

(Printed and published by Queensland Newspapers Pty Ltd of Campbell Street, Bowen Hills, Brisbane at that address. Registered by Australia Post — Publication No. QBF0420, and registered as a publication at the British Post Office.)

Prince Not Deterred By 'Danger' On Plane

NZPA   London

The Prince and Princess of Wales flew in an aircraft considered by its captain to be "potentially dangerous."

They made the flight because they did not wish to disappoint thousands of people who had turned out to see them in Victoria, says a British Press Association correspondent, Grania Forbes.

Prince Charles knew of the danger and made the decision to fly but he did not tell Princess Diana.

The aircraft's flaps jammed as it brought the royal couple in to land at the small town of Bendigo and it circled for several minutes before the crew were able to lower the flaps manually.

The same problem happened when the plane, a British-built HS748 turbo-prop, arrived at Ballarat to pick up the Prince and Princess for the journey. But Prince Charles, an experienced pilot, made the decision that they would fly in the plane.

The duty officer at the Royal Australian Air Force base at Fairbairn, Barry Cunstance, said: "The plane was to be positioned at Ballarat. It ran into problems with the flaps and spent 20 minutes in the air while the flaps were wound down manually before it could land.

"When it was on the ground the captain thought it not prudent to carry passengers. He considered it a potentially dangerous aircraft. The plane was considered insecure."

But the press officer for the royal couple, Mr Victor Chapman, said there was "no anxiety, no problem and no danger."

Prince Charles and Princess Diana responding with smiles to the welcome from the public at Auckland International Airport yesterday.

A bare-footed Prince William taking in the pomp and ceremony as he is carried to a waiting car on arrival at the airport yesterday.

Red Tape Cut As Royal Couple Warm to Crowd

The Prince of Wales broke through the red tape of a formal welcome to New Zealand by introducing Princess Diana to thousands of Aucklanders yesterday.

The move took royal tour officials and bodyguards by surprise as the royal couple swerved around their intended path to have their first close-up look at Princess Diana.

So unplanned was the gesture that the Commissioner of Police, Mr R. J. Walton, found himself heavily involved in "crowd control"—normally the duty of constables—as photographers swooped to record the Princess' first meeting with New Zealanders.

Journalists were shooed out of the way as the royal couple walked to the crowd to give New Zealanders their first close-up look at Princess Diana.

Irony

Ironically the first people the royal couple spoke to were British—although all now live in New Zealand.

None had ever seen royalty "at home" and did not seem to mind at all the irony of a few hours' wait in blustery conditions at an airport 12,000 miles away to have their first encounter of a close kind.

A Mangere bridge resident, Mrs Jessie Lee, who lived for more than 20 years in Manchester, suddenly found herself shaking hands and chatting with the Prince of Wales.

"I welcomed him to New Zealand and I told him his wife was very beautiful. He said 'Thank you,'" Mrs Lee said.

Said her 13-year-old son, Robert: "He (Prince Charles) has got quite a dark tan. I thought he would be all white."

Lovely

Mrs Sheila Jenkins, also formerly of Manchester, left her South Auckland home at 1 pm yesterday for the airport and "couldn't believe her eyes" when she found herself face-to-face with the royal couple.

"Prince Charles asked me if he had brought the bad weather with him. I told him I thought Princess Diana was just lovely and he said he thought so too," she said.

Another woman, who did not want to be named, waved an old photograph of Prince Charles meeting her in the 1960s when he came to New Zealand during his schooldays in Australia.

Changed

The old snap attracted Princess Diana's attention.

"She (Princess Diana) said: 'Darling, come here and have a look at this.'"

The Princess had observed that the old photograph made Prince Charles look like "your youngest brother" (Prince Edward). He had replied: "I've changed a lot since then . . . probably for the worse."

In spite of the impromptu meeting with the royal parents, the crowd caught only a glimpse of little Prince William as he was bundled down the stairs of the aircraft into a waiting car.

Salute

At that moment, a 21-gun artillery salute began but royal tour officials said later the little Prince remained completely undisturbed by the noisy gunnery.

It was all part of a much more formal welcome for the royal couple than was normally the case in their just-completed tour of Australia.

As the wind gusted and the rain threatened to fall the Prince and Princess were introduced to a long line of dignitaries — including members of the cabinet — who had earlier stood uncomfortably on the tarmac awaiting the arrival of the royal aircraft.

But once the formalities were over the royal couple — perhaps setting the tone for what is to be a rigidly organised tour — headed to meet the people.

Some they did not meet were in a group of pro-testers. Police were at the airport in strength to ensure the royal tour did not get off to a nasty start.

They were hardly needed. The protesters were halted at the gate leading to the public viewing enclosure and the Prince and Princess would not have heard a word from their loudhailers.

The band of about 80 to 100 protesters was well-behaved although one man, using a loudhailer, told the crowd: "These royal bludgers will not do us any good. When they go home there will still be high unemployment here."

The protesters carried banners condemning the Treaty of Waitangi, British involvement in Northern Ireland, anti-royal slogans and even one proclaiming Argentina's right to the Falkland Islands.

As the royal couple arrived the group split up. They reunited shortly afterwards and, in scenes reminiscent of the 1981 Springbok rugby tour, they were closely flanked by police officers as they marched around surrounding streets.

Traffic Jam

But the day belonged to the New Zealanders who turned out to see the royal couple — and many made no secret of the fact they were there to see the Princess above all.

About 1100 watched the royal motorcade passed through Otahuhu and a further 3000 lined the roads near Government House in Epsom to catch a glimpse of the famous couple.

But nowhere was there greater delight than among those who got their first close look at the Princess.

Perhaps less overjoyed were those caught up in a massive traffic jam which followed the procession of official vehicles. The single file of traffic from the airport to Kirkbride Rd was at a standstill for almost 30 minutes and remained at a snail's pace on most routes leading to the Southern Motorway.

● More pictures, back page; today's programme, page 3.

STRIKES FUTURE CLOUDED

Union meetings at two of the country's industrial troublespots will be held this morning, although it was not clear last night whether they would pave the way for settlements.

At Kawerau, about 630 pulp and paper workers at the Tasman mill will meet at 8 am to review their strike which began a week ago.

And at the Marsden Pt oil refinery extensions project, 600 striking riggers and labourers, whose action has led to widespread suspensions of other workers, will also meet.

However, there did not appear to be much hope of a return to work at Kawerau.

The president of the Northern Federation of Pulp and Paper Workers, Mr J. H. Morgan, said yesterday that he could not see a return to work unless the company made further offers on the federation's log of claims.

The workers have struck in protest at Tasman's offers on a number of allowance and condition payments in their award, although they have settled on a basic 10 per cent wage rise.

Meanwhile, some of the 100 forestry workers employed by the Kaingaroa Logging Company, a Tasman subsidiary, will be suspended tomorrow and Wednesday unless the dispute is resolved.

At Marsden Pt, more than 400 workers were suspended last week as the effects of the labourers' strike took effect.

The labourers will meet this morning to consider developments in the dispute over the recruitment policies of the Joint Venture II consortium.

And in another industrial dispute 150 members of the Rotowaro branch of the New Zealand Engine Drivers' Union have begun a series of rolling stoppages at the state coal mines at Huntly and Rotowaro.

They have done so in protest at the refusal of the Government to allow the establishment of a committee to investigate their pay relativities with similar workers in other industries.

WOMAN RAPED

A 75-year-old Ngaruawahia woman was raped shortly after retiring to bed at 9.30 last night.

Senior Sergeant Brian Walters, of the Hamilton police, said the offender entered her home through a bedroom window.

No description was available of the offender early this morning. Hamilton police were continuing their investigations.

Two Killed In Copter Crash

A Taupo pilot and his passenger died when the helicopter they were in crashed soon after take-off from a private farm near Taupo at 8.10 pm yesterday.

They were Mr Joseph Charles Keeley, aged 35, and Miss Rose Westerman, aged 22, also of Taupo.

Perfect Princess Quick To Meet Her Fans

The Princess of Wales arrived in New Zealand looking just as her fans expected — perfect.

In fact, not a hair of her South Kensington-created hairdo moved while Prince Charles and others battled to control sometimes unruly hair and flapping ties.

The Princess looked slim and elegant in a full-skirted cream wool dress with a fitted waist and a double row of light brown buttons down the front.

The wide collar and cuffs, and a neat hat, were also trimmed with brown. She carried a black handbag and wore matching shoes.

The 1.78-metre (5ft 10in) tall Princess Diana wore her hemline several inches below those of the row of waiting VIP wives — a length she favours.

Whether it was the heat of the aircraft's interior or too much blusher, her face appeared flushed as she chatted animatedly to the Governor-General's wife, Lady Beattie, throughout the welcoming ceremony.

Princess Diana continued to look perfect, smile and chat as she moved down the line of eagerly waiting dignitaries, clasping her hands together between each handshake.

But it was when she reached high for the outstretched hands of "Princess Di" fans who had waited for hours behind a barrier that her face really came to life.

She laughed, talked and joked while the lucky ones peered at her skin and those famous eyes, clicked their camera lenses and eyed her huge sapphire and diamond engagement ring.

It was Prince Charles who in the end intervened by gently steering his wife towards the waiting Rolls-Royce with his hand cupped in the small of her back.

A suntanned Prince William gave waiting dignitaries a rather startled look as he was hurried down the steps from the aircraft in the arms of his nanny, Miss Barbara Barnes.

The sudden appearance of the solid-looking, fair-haired baby was a plus for waiting photographers who could not decide whether to focus on the Prince and Princess of Wales or on the precious bundle in Miss Barnes' arms.

Wearing a pale orange romper suit and a white cardigan, the bare-legged Prince William was taken straight to a waiting car especially fitted with a child safety seat for the journey to Government House.

He sat wide-eyed during the Royal New Zealand Air Force's 21 gun salute and waited patiently while his parents shook hands with VIPs and members of the waiting crowd.

Prince William apparently took an instant liking to the Government House nursery where he will spend the next two weeks, and to a white rabbit dressed in an All Black shirt which was waiting to greet him.

Photographers and journalists will gather at Government House this morning for a brief photographic session with the baby prince.

Vanishing Vehicles Tally 7000

The number of unrecovered motor vehicles in the Auckland police district has topped 7000 — and police say the total is growing by about 100 a month.

The total includes 2200 motorcycles and hundreds of cheaper early model cars.

But the recovery rate for stolen vehicles, the police say, is still considerably higher than it is for other stolen property.

Police records show, however, that there were 7000 vehicles listed as "unrecovered" at the end of March.

Stealing cars is a high turnover crime. In the Auckland police district last year 9409 motor vehicles were taken — about 26 a day.

But Detective Senior Sergeant M. I. Whittam, of the Auckland Central car squad, said 77 per cent of those vehicles were recovered.

Many of those vehicles were stolen before 1982 and are likely to have been reduced to scrap metal and spare parts.

Senior Sergeant Whittam said most vehicles stolen were cheaper cars — early model Cortinas and Minis were typical targets — and many ended up with back-yard wreckers.

There was a ready market for older spare parts because many were no longer made.

Sergeant P. A. Mildenhull said the value of motor vehicles stolen in the Auckland police district last year was just over $20.1 million.

Vehicles valued at about $15.5 million were recovered.

But of the other property valued at $25 million stolen in Auckland, goods worth only about $2.5 million were recovered by the police.

Sergeant Mildenhall said that several years ago probably about 99 per cent of vehicles stolen were taken for a joyride and then abandoned. Consequently, the recovery rate was high.

But of the other property, the recovery rate was low.

That was the reason for a lower recovery rate.

Marathon Win

NZPA-Reuter   London

Mike Gratton, of Britain, the Commonwealth Games bronze medallist, won the London marathon yesterday in an unofficial time of two hours nine minutes 44 seconds.

Charles & Diana in Canada

For 17 days in June and one special Canada Day, the Prince and Princess of Wales captivated the nation on their first royal visit. This is The Star's — and your — pictorial souvenir section.

STAR PHOTOS BY DAVID COOPER

Anthony Holden was born in Lancashire in 1947. He has enjoyed a distinguished journalistic career in Fleet Street and as an author. He won the Pfizer Young Journalist of the Year Award in 1972, was commended in the British Press Awards of 1976, and in 1977 was named Columnist of the Year for his work as the diarist Atticus in the London *Sunday Times*. This last award was presented by Prince Charles, who said "He thoroughly deserves it … His style is most enjoyable — witty, amusing, slightly sardonic … His English is a pleasure to read."
His books include *Charles, Prince of Wales* and *Their Royal Highnesses,* which was published to mark the wedding of Prince Charles and Lady Diana Spencer in 1981.
He lived in Washington, D.C., as chief U.S. correspondent for *The Observer* from 1979 to 1981, when he returned to London to become assistant editor of *The Times*. Having resigned in 1982, he is now a prolific freelance journalist, broadcaster and author.
He lives in London with his wife Amanda and three young sons.

Acknowledgements: The publishers wish to thank Mr John Frost for his research, and for access to his newspaper collection. We also wish to acknowledge the following organisations for permission to reproduce their front pages: Mirror Group Newspapers Ltd for the *Daily Mirror, Sunday Mirror* and *Sunday Pictorial*; Associated Newspapers Group PLC for the *Daily Mail, Daily Sketch, News Chronicle, The Star* and *Evening News*; Express Newspapers PLC for the *Daily Express, Evening Standard* and *Daily Star*; The International Thomson Organisation PLC for the *Daily Graphic* and *Sunday Graphic*; and News International PLC for *The Sun*. Thanks also to the publishers of the *Newcastle Evening Chronicle, The South Wales Echo, New Zealand Herald, Melbourne Herald, Toronto Star, The Times* of Swaziland, *The Illustrated London News,* and the proprietors of other newspapers featured in this book.